THE CREAKY TRAVELER
In the North West Highlands of Scotland

THE CREAKY TRAVELER

IN THE NORTH WEST HIGHLANDS OF SCOTLAND

A Journey for the Mobile but Not Agile

WARREN ROVETCH

SENTIENT PUBLICATIONS, LLC

First Sentient Publications edition 2002
Copyright © 2002 by Warren Rovetch

Printed in Canada

The Creaky Traveler is a registered trademark of Warren Rovetch.

Cover design by Kim Johansen, Black Dog Design
Book design by Rudy J.Ramos, Rudy Ramos Design Studio
Maps and calligraphy by Alison Richards

Library of Congress Cataloging-in-Publication Data

Rovetch, Warren.
The creaky traveler in the north west highlands of scotland : a
journey for the mobile but not agile / Warren Rovetch.-- 1st Sentient
Publications ed.
p. cm.
ISBN 0-9710786-7-X
1. Highlands (Scotland)--Description and travel. 2. Rovetch,
Warren--Journeys--Scotland--Highlands. I. Title.
DA880.H7 R65 2002
914.11'5--dc21
2002007219

SENTIENT PUBLICATIONS
A Limited Liability Company
1113 Spruce Street
Boulder, CO 80302
www.sentientpublications.com

To G
whom I love very much

CONTENTS

ACKNOWLEDGMENTS

THIS BOOK WOULD NOT have been possible without the help of many people. First, of course, there is my dear wife G, a Creaky Traveler in her own right, whose sensitive observations and insights inform much of this book. As a reader of various drafts, she kept me out of serious trouble. My three daughters, Lissa Rovetch, Emily Whitman, and Jennifer Rovetch, all of whom got higher marks in English than I ever did, tried to make sure my sentences didn't go on forever and that I didn't ride certain hobby horses too long. Their enthusiasm for what I wrote helped move me along. Fathers can never get enough praise from their daughters.

Several friends read drafts, and their comments, reflecting various perspectives, made an important contribution to the end result. This hardy group included Charles Wilkinson, law professor and author, who had deadlines of his own to meet; Ann Guthrie, a wonderful potter and precise editor; Tom Woodard, teacher, writer, and a most exacting reader of drafts; Margaret Sugar, a world traveler of consequence; and Donald Laing, whose observations and personal lending library were most helpful.

And then there is George Sugar, whose patient instruction and computer magic made it possible for this cyber illiterate to get from one end of the book to the other. Pages would disappear, the computer would stop in its tracks, the printer would go dead. Sometimes a house call was required, but more often than not a phone call to George was all it took for the computer to behave.

Two Scotsmen, Hugh Maclellan and Donald Grant, were generous with their time and sharing of family backgrounds, going back hundreds of years. They helped bring a personal dimension to Highlands history. Donald MacLeod, editor of *Am Bratach*, news magazine for the North West Highlands, was invaluable in helping me avoid mistakes on Gaelic matters and locate sources and in providing the names of Gaelic experts. Thanks to Fiona McKenzie and Brenda Mearns, you will know how to pronounce Achilltibuie, Kylesku, and a couple dozen other Gaelic place names. Graham Bruce, head teacher of Durness Primary School, and Dr. Ian Smith, rector (principal) of Kinlochbervie High School, provided me with contemporary insights into Scottish education. Rita Hunter, manager of Feis Rois, was generous in opening doors to a wonderful occasion of traditional music.

Erica Gorman deserves special note. Thousands of toads owe their lives to Erica, organizer and leader of the Toad Patrol at Loch Ordain. I owe Erica a great debt for her patient explanations of the wiles and ways of spawning toads, one of the more important stories you will find in this book.

I can't leave Scotland without a special thanks to the able innkeepers whose warmth, hospitality, and good eats contributed mightily to needs of body and soul—Di Johnson and Inge Ford of Little Lodge, Gerry and Mark Irvine of Summer Isles Hotel, Lesley Crosfield and Colin Craig of Albannach, and Lesley Black of Port-Na-Con.

I also want to acknowledge several authors whom I met only through their writing and whose work was of special importance to my understanding of Scottish character and history and the events that formed them.

- T. M. Devine, author of *The Scottish Nation* 1700-2000 (2000). Devine is Director of the Research Institute of Irish and Scottish Studies at the University of Aberdeen. Reviewers have called this book "a fiercely intelligent account of Scotland" and "the work of a compendious historical mind." It is all of that.
- James R. Baldwin, editor of *Peoples and Settlement in North-West Ross* (1994). This book probes the past and present of communities in the Atlantic coastal area we traveled. It offers a richness of detail

only serious academic research can provide. Especially relevant sections were the "Preface," by John R. Baldwin; "Ullapool and the British Fisheries Society," by Jean Munro; and "'Locals' and 'Incomers': Social and Cultural Identity in Late Twentieth Century Coigach," by Angus MacLeod and Geoff Payne.

- John MacAskill, author of *We Have Won the Land* (1999). This account of the crofters' purchase of "their" land opened a window to the past in Assynt, one of the areas we traveled, and to the meaning of a land reform debate that is going on in the Scottish Parliament as this is written.

- Katharine Stewart, author of *Crofts and Crofting* (1996). The title says it all—the origin, evolution, issues, and values associated with crofts and crofting, and a brilliantly concise presentation that "put me in the picture."

- Rob Humphreys and Donald Reid, authors of *Scottish Highlands & Islands: The Rough Guide* (2000). An exceedingly well-written guidebook of substance and strong opinions by writers who know the territory. They filled in many gaps for me.

- Brian Bell, editor of *Scotland: Insight Guide* (1995). Concise, erudite, and pithy insights into the Scottish character, the influence of the church, and the making of modern Scotland.

- Ronald Lansley, compiler of *Durness Past and Present* (1998). A wonderfully personal collection of records and reminiscences by the people of the Parish of Durness, the northwest corner of Scotland, and Great Britain.

Acknowledgements would not be complete without my considerable thanks to Connie Shaw, Sentient Publications editor and book doctor, without whom none of this would now be read.

WARREN ROVETCH
The Creaky Traveler
Boulder, Colorado
July 2002

The Three Worlds of Scotland—
Lowlands, Highlands & Beyond

ATLANTIC OCEAN

Atlantic
Highlands

Population Density:
Persons per square mile
England 949
Scotland
    Lowlands 266
    Highlands 21
    Atlantic Highlands . . . 1

Inverness

Highlands

SCOTLAND

NORTH SEA

Lowlands

Edinburgh

ENGLAND

WALES

London

N

0   50
miles

AR

INTRODUCTION

THIS BOOK HAS SEVERAL goals. One, as the title suggests, is to explain and demonstrate how Creaky Travelers, the growing ranks of the mobile but not agile, can plan and manage successful independent travel. My wife Gerda (who prefers to be called "G") and I, both of advanced years, have been on twenty-five or so trips of three weeks each or more to all parts of Europe. While the scope of what we can manage has grown less over time (we walk, but not very much; we climb stairs, but not too many), our capacity to find meaning and enjoyment has grown. Less can be more. With good research, proper planning, and an understanding of assistance readily available from airlines and others, any Creaky Traveler can satisfy needs of body and soul.

Another goal is to share with you our experiences and our feelings as we explored Britain's last wilderness, the Atlantic coastal region of the North West Highlands of Scotland. There were many special people and places. To put you in the picture, here is a map showing the border between England and Scotland, the division between Scottish Highlands and Lowlands, and the area of the Atlantic coastal region of the North West Highlands we traveled through. I love maps, so there are a number of them in this book. When I share a special place with you, I want you to know where it is and add photographs to give you a feel of the place.

Our journey took us north along the stark, rugged, and mysteriously beautiful coast of Wester Ross and North West Sutherland as far north as it is possible to go. We traveled remote, winding, single-track (one lane) roads, driving carefully and slowly to avoid sheep and new-born lambs that claim the right of way. A succession of deep sea lochs reach in from the Atlantic to define the crenellated coast—Loch Gairloch, Loch Ewe (where World War II convoys assembled for desperate runs to Murmansk), Little Loch Broom, Loch Broom, Loch Inver, and Loch Eriboll. The peaks of An Teallach, Suilven, Assynt, Ben Moore, and Ben Hope rise abruptly one by one from their base, punctuating long views over heather-clad moors. This is sit-and-stare country. It has a quality that empties the mind, touches the soul, and lets the good stuff in.

The places we stayed were memorable. We chose small guesthouses, each with a distinctive personality and great views. Proprietor chefs who took great pride in their use of free range and locally grown ingredients ran the guesthouses. Also, when planning the trip, we wanted to make sure we stayed where we wouldn't mind settling in on a rainy day. And so we stayed three days at each stop, allowing for plenty of time to wander and wonder. These stops were not more than one-and-a-half or two hours apart. We have three rules for moving on: leave plenty of time to pause and inhale views along the way, get to the next stop and get settled in by early afternoon, and don't get there tired. With single-track roads, sheep, and sights to see along the way, the distance driven between stops might be only thirty to forty miles, but the change in character of the scenery is often dramatic.

Wherever we wandered, there was one pervasive feature—the remains of stone croft houses, reminders of a way of life reaching back as far as three hundred years. Next to many of these stone remains were new, whitewashed homes built with state subsidies that cover fifty percent or more of the cost. An array of other subsidies cover fence building, drainage, farm equipment, and a dozen other categories. They are designed to support crofting as a way of life and sustain the social and cultural fabric of this area of the Highlands.

This takes us to the third goal of the book. It is to place our trip and our experiences in the economic, social, and cultural context of

Scotland and the Atlantic Highlands. A rising tide of nationalism beginning in the 1970s led to "devolution of powers" and the election in 1999 of a Scottish Parliament—Scotland's first since 1707, when the Treaty of Union incorporated the Scottish Parliament into the Westminster Parliament. Few Scots ever fully accepted this "shotgun marriage" and sing of it as a time "we were bought and sold for English gold." With devolution Scotland became one of four states comprising the United Kingdom along with Wales, Northern Ireland, and England. Not to shrink from Scotland's new "independence," Henry McLeish, First Minister (Scotland's prime minister), speaks of Scotland as "our nation . . . a modern dynamic country." He spelled out the new responsibility of Scotland's government for "the issues of day-to-day concern to people of Scotland, including health, education, justice, rural affairs, and transport, [and] an annual budget of around £20 billion ($35 billion)."

Historian T. M. Devine calls this period following devolution, "A time when Scotland is entering a phase of historic constitutional change when issues such as identity and culture are being reclaimed." Talking about these changing times, Di Johnson, proprietor of Little Lodge in North Erradale, put it well when she spoke of "living with echoes of the past and winds of the future." It remains to be seen whether the winds will be gentle breezes or gale force. Whichever, the further north we traveled, the surer we were that Scotland is not just a different kind of England.

THREE WORLDS: LOWLANDS, HIGHLANDS, AND BEYOND

LONDON TO DURNESS AT the northern tip of Scotland is a distance of only 650 miles, but in the style and content of life it is worlds away. The differences are more than ones of degree. Life in Durness and other areas of the Atlantic Highlands is of a different kind. First there are the Lowlands, home to ninety-six percent of Scotland's five million people, virtually all of Scotland's manufacturing, several world-class universities, and the urban centers of Glasgow (pop. 682,500) and Edinburgh (pop. 504,500). The population density of the Lowlands is 266 people per square mile, compared with 949 in England.

Another statistic of meaning may be the number of distilleries on the Whiskey Trail. Between the Lowlands and the Highlands there are no fewer than 122 distilleries on the trail, beginning with Alberfeldy, passing through familiar ones like Glenfiddich and Sheep Dip, and ending with Tullibardine. On April 17, 2002, a bottle of Macallan 60-year-old single malt sold at McTear's auction house in Glasgow for £20,150 ($30,670). According to the BBC, "The buyer will be able to specify the design of a bespoke [custom-made] label for the bottle."

Moving north, the Highlands define the second world. It has only four percent of Scotland's population in a little over thirty-three percent of Scotland's 28,260 square miles. The population density is only twenty-one men, women, and children per square mile, less than a tenth of Lowlands' density. Most of the Highlands population is concentrated in the rich farmlands and charming villages along the eastern seaboard, including Inverness, capital of the Highlands. With 50,900 people, Inverness accounts for a quarter of all 206,900 Highlanders. Dornoch lies a bit north of Inverness, and, according to *The Rough Guide*, it is "a middle-class holiday resort with solid Edwardian hotels, trees and flowers in profusion, and miles of sandy beaches." Dornoch used to be renowned for its championship golf course (ranked eleventh in the world) and is the place where, in 1722, the last burning of a witch in Scotland took place. It is now benefiting, some may say suffering, from the "Madonna Effect." Since Madonna and British film director Guy Richie got married to worldwide publicity at Skibo Castle on the Dornoch Firth, couples searching for castle rooms and romance have swamped Dornoch and its neighbors. A room for two at Skibo goes for £700 ($1,015) a night, with meals and services extra. Concerned about space? Not to worry, there are fifty rooms.

And then there is the very different third world of Scotland, the western coast of Wester Ross and Sutherland. For purposes of this book, I refer to this narrow sliver at the northwest corner of Scotland that G and I traveled as the Atlantic Highlands. Most sources lump the east and west coasts at the north end of the Highlands together and call the whole of it the North West Highlands. But since the east and west coasts are fundamentally different in character and approaches to life, I feel this further division is called for.

The Atlantic Highlands begin at the relatively gentle shores of Loch Gairloch, and as you move north, the country is increasingly romantic, moody, raw, uncompromising, timeless, and isolated. The density is one person per square mile. Most people live in crofting townships—clusters of five to ten homes. The largest village in the area has a population of around six hundred, and primary schools, grades one through seven, enroll twenty-five to thirty students. From where our travels along the coast began in Gairloch to Durness where our travels ended a month later, the distance, as the crow flies, is about 65 miles. By main roads it is 130 miles. By our route it was nearly 200 miles. If you took a boat and followed the ins and outs of Loch Ewe, Little Loch Broom, Annat Bay, Enard Bay, Loch Inver, and all the other bays and sea lochs, you would cover well over a thousand miles of coastline.

"ANCIENT AND SIGNIFICANT MEANING"

THE DIVISION BETWEEN HIGHLAND and Lowland Scots once ran very deep. Noblemen with attitudes and values of the English ruling class controlled the Lowlands. The Highlands remained untamed until the 1700s, when clan chiefs began to see economic and social advantages in better relations with the Lowlands and with England. Clans controlled territories that were virtual kingdoms. Peasants lived in communal groupings, and bloody feuds between clans were a regular feature of clan life. Lowlanders viewed the Highlands as "a savage and untamed nation." Time and tide eroded most of the Highland/Lowland distinctions, except along the Atlantic coastal area of Wester Ross and Sutherland. About life in this small territory, traveled historian T. C. Smout writes, "The ancient and significant meaning of being a Highlander is very much alive."

The social and cultural fabric of these Highlanders has been shaped largely by four forces—collective memory of The Clearances, a cooperative style of life in crofting townships, Presbyterianism that puts ordinary people in direct touch with God, and an abiding love and respect for the land.

In the early 1800s, in what became known as The Clearances, large landowners used unnecessarily cruel methods to clear families from fertile valleys to make way for more profitable sheep. Many families were "cleared" to America, Canada, and Australia—a Scottish diaspora that has produced today a world community of twenty million Scots outside of Scotland, and global industries in tartans, Highland games, and searches of family genealogy. Other North West Highland families were cleared to "crofts" on marginal lands along the Atlantic seaboard. Crofts were (and are) small parcels of a few acres each for a home, garden crops, and rights to graze a few cattle or sheep on nearby hills. By design, crofts seldom provided enough food for survival, forcing crofters to seek "cash" work, frequently for the landlord who had cleared them. Crofts were clustered in crofting townships where mutual help and cooperation were the rule. This communal style of life, rooted in the heritage of clan living, was essential to survival. Mutual help and cooperation are still the basic characteristics of township living. The instinct for "community" is also rooted in a divine right to be an individualist.

According to novelist Naomi May, since in the Presbyterian Church of Scotland ordinary people can be in direct touch with God, no man or woman is better than the next. "The relationship between the individual soul to his or her Maker put emphasis on self reliance and personal integrity—essentials for survival in a poor country with a harsh climate." This directness, the belief that people are equal in the eyes of their Lord, finds its way into everyday dealings, opinions, and likes and dislikes.

Combine these forces and today, according to Smout, you find in the Atlantic Highlands a people and a society "often unmodern in priorities, materialistic yet with little sense of individual ambition . . . supportive of its members, [that] has an abiding sense of kinship and an unembarrassed love of song and story." Smout adds it also has "an unembarrassed love of drink." He should also have added "a deep and abiding love of their land" wrested at great human cost from wretched beginnings, made productive, and now preserved with respect—not a junk car or trash heap in sight.

OFF AND MEANDERING

BEYOND THE PROSPECT OF great natural beauty and good access for Creaky Travelers to remote places, it was anticipation of this world of ancient and significant meaning and uncommon people that took us to the Highlands. It turned out there was a bonus feature on this trip we hadn't anticipated. It was a sense of safety. We were not on guard. For a month, the world was not dangerous. In G's words, "I never felt uneasy." No matter how remote or isolated a place or lively a pub, "I never had a sense that anyone was bent on harm."

So here we go on our journey of discovery—off and meandering!

NOTES ON PRONUNCIATION

SEVERAL OF THE GAELIC place names used in the text are followed by their English pronunciation – or rather, a best effort at this. One problem is that the Gaelic sound "ch" does not exist in English. In the text the sound is represented by the letter combination "hh." Example: loch (lake) = lohh, not lock. Try the hh sound while breathing out and with a little gargle. Or try the German "ach" as if it was in the non-word lawchful.

Also, in Gaelic, the first syllable of a word almost always gets the emphasis. Example: Durness, not Durness. There are a few exceptions as in Lochinver, but not many. Additional information on Gaelic pronunciation is provided in Appendix III.

* * *

In this book, Celtic knots appear below the title of each chapter as decoration. Speculation has it that similar knotwork decorating many seventh to ninth century Celtic Christian manuscripts was symbolic of the interconnectedness and continuity of life.

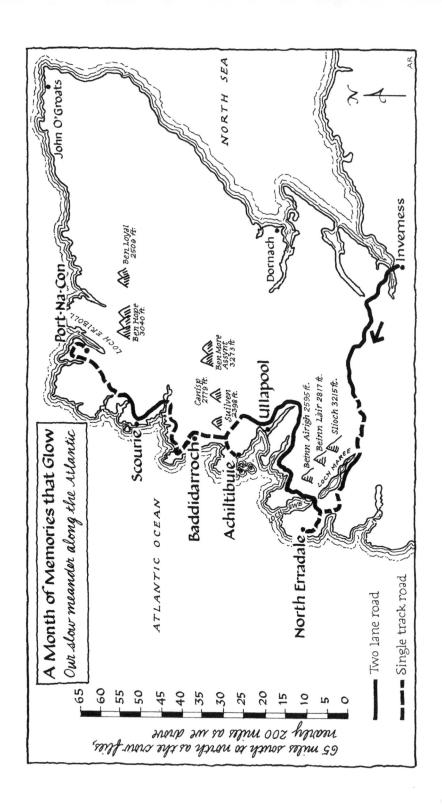

A Month of Memories that Glow

Our slow meander along the Atlantic

John O'Groats

NORTH SEA

Ben Loyal
2509 ft.

Ben Hope
3040 ft.

Dornach

Inverness

Port·Na·Con

LOCH ERIBOLL

Ben More
Assynt
3273 ft.

Canisp
2779 ft.

Suilven
2398 ft.

Ullapool

Scourie

Baddidarroch

Benn Airigh 2595 ft.

Benn Làir 2817 ft.

Slioch 3215 ft.

LOCH MAREE

Achiltibuie

LOCH EWE

ATLANTIC OCEAN

North Erradale

Two lane road

Single track road

65 70 60 55 50 45 40 35 30 25 20 15 10 5 0

65 miles south to north as the crow flies,
nearly 200 miles as we drove

AR

N

PART I
A JOURNEY OF DISCOVERY

CHAPTER ONE

REFLECTIONS

Cuir culaib cuir culaibh
> Turning your back, turning your back

Cuir cul ri tir nan Gaidheal
> Turning your back on the land of the Highlander

Ach duil gu 'n till mi dhachaidh ann
> But I hope to return there

SOUL FOOD

AT THE BEGINNING OF our trip, the Gaelic songs we played as we drove along were music to our ears. Before long, this music touched our souls. If you don't have a spiritual side, the sights and sounds of the Highlands will help you grow one. If you have a spiritual side, the Highlands will most certainly nourish it. Soul food is all around.

My wife Gerda (G) and I agree—this was the best trip we have ever taken, creaky or not. We know it brought us a sense of peace and well-being. We laughed a lot, saw breathtakingly wonderful country, and ate and slept well in delightful guest houses. But what were the things that really made our Highland experience so personal and so different?

For most of our trip we were at the edge of the sea. Mountains were always in view as we moved north slowly from North Erradale to Ullapool, Achiltibuie, Baddidarroch, Scourie, and Port-Na-Con. Early on we realized we were in a very different world than any we had known before. This world looked different, felt different, acted different, and had its own priorities and imperatives. And it was open to us not as observers, but as participants.

We had the feeling of an intimate relationship with the natural world. It began the first evening at Little Lodge when a brilliant double rainbow began its high arch fifty feet from where we sat. For most of the trip, there was nothing between us and the raw beauty of bogs and mountains and rugged sea lochs. And mostly, we didn't have to share it. This made it a very personal relationship. And we didn't have to drive through anything bad to get to what was good, like braving the industrial wasteland of Padua to get to the old city.

Virtually all the man-made buildings and tracks in the area we covered seemed to grow out of the land and fit together in peaceful harmony—rubble walls of abandoned croft houses, weathered fences, neat white cottages. The small villages and crofting townships are not preserved and prettified. There were few discordant notes to jar our senses. No billboards, neon signs, or drive-ins. No slums, no junk cars.

In their relationships people are direct and equal. We were never fawned over or patronized. Clerk in the village store, barkeep, guest house proprietor, waitress, bank teller, or school headmaster—it is clear from the way people carry themselves and deal with each other that no person feels better than the next.

People of all ages retain the ability to entertain each other, in part because they share great pleasure in music, dance, and poetry. They cooperate willingly in community matters (including saving toads) and have an abiding concern for education of the young. Preschool is universal, which is not surprising in a society that had near-universal elementary education in the eighteenth century.

SHARP CONTRASTS

WHATEVER THE ROOT SOURCE—clans, church, density—the non-material and locally significant values and qualities of life in the Highlands are real and palpable. What makes these qualities stand out so sharply for me is their contrast with the not-all-bad, market driven values of American society. Social observers view the 1990s as the "me decade," the era of instant millionaires and heightened material gratification when everything worth having seemed to have a price and the booming economy seemed to have no end. The 1990s and early 2000s in America also saw a blurring, some say erosion, of the traditional values that remain so much in evidence in the Highlands—duty, compassion, community, and loyalty. Donald Kennedy, president emeritus of Stanford University, has written about the college market in which academic stars sell their wares to the highest bidder. "There are all kinds of loyalties and the institutional kind no longer trumps the others. . . . What happened to loyalty is that it has been broken up into a lot of pieces in a highly complex world. But I confess I rather liked the old world in which loyalty was easier to keep track of." Perhaps Dr. Kennedy would like to try the Highlands.

I wonder if what reached us so deeply in the Highlands is that as a society and an economy, the northern communities along the Atlantic seaboard haven't kept up with the rest of the world, or even with neighbors fifty miles away on the east coast of the North West Highlands. In the end this is precisely what may put them ahead. John Baldwin, who has studied the culture and the economy of the area, defines it as pastoral, "supported by modest farming, fishing and woodland management . . . often recognized nowadays as environmentally as well as culturally sympathetic—role models perhaps for a new era of lower key sustainable lifestyles."

That lifestyle in its Highland setting is what so captivated G and me.

MEMORIES THAT GLOW

WE HAVE MANY INDELIBLE memories of the Highlands. Here are a few of the scenes you will find in the pages ahead.

Pure Magic. Morning mist burning off the Summer Isles and the opalescent, shimmering evening light there.

Best View from a Bedroom Window. Suilven seen across Loch Inver from our room at the Albannach.

Never Even Imagined Before Sight. The seabird high-rise on the cliffs of Handa Island.

Best Walk. A dappled morning in a willow wood along the falls and pools and swirls of the River Inver (G inventing book titles—*The Cornstarch Affair* and *Three Jolly Butchers and a Chicken*—and collapsing with laughter).

Never Seen Before. At Little Lodge, a perfect double rainbow rising from the pasture fifty feet from where we stood, completing its arc on a far hillside.

Most Dreamy Scene. Along the shores of Loch Raa, over the crest of the moor, and looking across a golden valley, the first sight of the Summer Isles in Badentarbet Bay and the Hebrides beyond.

Best Technicolor Scene. At Tarbet, an orange and purple sunset piercing black clouds gathering over the Sound of Handa.

Most Touching. Loch Ewe—snow white newborn lambs lying in high green grass at mother's feet, some lambs struggling to stand.

Most Confounding. "Toad Crossing" warning at Lochan Ordain.

Best Picnic Place. Looking up at Stoer Lighthouse and down to the crashing sea.

Best Single Dish. Thai shrimp in an Altandhu pub.

Greatest Cultural Impact. Feis Rois, Gaelic music workshop and impromptu "sessions" at The Ceilidh Place.

Most Striking Color. Clachtoll Beach—turquoise water, green grass, yellow sand and rust colored rocks.

Most Dramatic. Storm clouds swirling around the peak of Ben Hope, roiling Loch Eriboll in the foreground.

Most Instructive. Pubkeeper's lecture on the evils of tap water because chlorine destroys the aroma and taste of decent scotch.

Most Riveting. Following the rear end of a Highland cow and her triplets for a half hour down a narrow track.

As you read about our journey of discovery, you will understand why G and I will return to the Highlands.

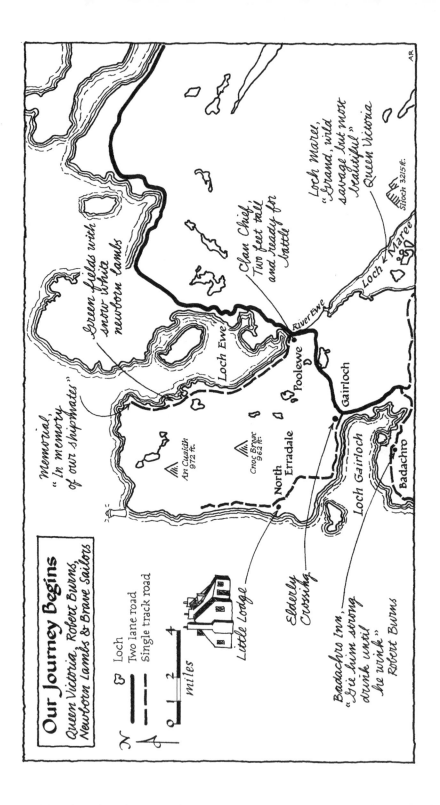

Our Journey Begins
Queen Victoria, Robert Burns,
Newborn Lambs & Brave Sailors

Loch

Two lane road

Single track road

miles
0 1 2 4

Memorial,
"In memory
of our shipmates"

Green fields with
snow white
newborn lambs

Clan Chief,
Two feet tall
and ready for
battle

Loch Maree,
"Grand, wild
savage but most
beautiful"
Queen Victoria

Slioch 3215 ft.

Loch Maree

River Ewe

Loch Ewe

Poolewe

Gairloch

An Cuaidh
972 ft.

Cnoc Breac
962 ft.

North
Erradale

Loch Gairloch

Badachro

Little Lodge

Elderly
Crossing

Badachro Inn,
"Gie him strong
drink until
he wink"
Robert Burns

AR

CHAPTER TWO

INVERNESS, LOCH MAREE, GAIRLOCH, POOLEWE

GETTING THERE PLEASED

OUR APPROACH IS TO ease into an overseas trip. The key is to start slow and not speed up too much along the way. The first test is the airport. At the beginning of May, G and I left Denver on British Airways at 6:25 P.M., nonstop to London (Gatwick), and arrived at 10:30 A.M. The elapsed time was nine hours, and the time change seven hours. After a four-hour layover we connected to Inverness, arriving at 4:45 P.M.

Leaving Denver I was reminded that large airports are factories, and their product is processing "stressed humanity" at the lowest possible unit cost. Long walks, lots of noise, rush, waiting in line to check in, and then being herded aboard with two to three hundred other souls are standard procedures and ordinarily part of being processed in. Fly a short night, land overseas at another big airport, and there are more long walks, lines at customs, and baggage scramble. Then you are processed out (how the Creaky Traveler retains sanity and manages all this is dealt with in the second section of this book). Denver International Airport (DIA) is big. It has three terminals and eighty-nine gates, and on an average day DIA handles 1,447 arriving and departing flights carrying 106,169 passengers. Gatwick is just a little smaller, with 83,315 passengers a day, most of them operating at a somewhat higher decibel level than those at DIA. So in chaos terms, it's a tie.

Then there is Inverness (Dalcross Airport), a sweetheart of an airport of very personal proportions—1,096 passengers a day, two gates, one arrival and one departure lobby, and never more than one plane at a time coming or going. Picture our arrival: We fly in low over open green fields, landing softly, walk down the airplane steps into the fresh air and sunshine, a hundred feet to the lobby, bags waiting at the single baggage carousel, then fifteen feet to the Hertz counter, and a hundred more feet to our car.

Twenty-five minutes (eight miles) later we parked in the middle of Inverness, along the river Ness, its banks covered with yellow spring daffodils. We arrived at Felstead House, our bed-and-breakfast, for the night. Proprietor Diarmid Troup welcomed us like long lost friends, and in three minutes we were in our cheerful room looking out a huge bay window at the river, with daffodils and church spires beyond, barely winded and very pleased with ourselves.

It was 5:30 P.M. (10:30 A.M. Denver time), and we had been on the road for about twenty-four hours. The trick for the first night is to stay in a comfortable place where the outlook is pleasant, and where you can get there and spend your first evening in an uncomplicated and undemanding way.

Our evening started with a cup of tea, then we went out for a slow stroll along the river, across a pedestrian bridge, and a meander upstream to Ness Bridge. Inverness Castle, its crenellated pink stone all floodlit, hovers on a hillside above the river. As royalty intended, the castle dominates the scene. We looked for Duncan's ghost along the way. Local lore has it that Duncan was murdered in Macbeth's eleventh-century castle downstream from Ness Bridge, and with the onset of night, Duncan's ghost walks the banks of the River Ness. A beautiful sunset, and dinner at the Riva, a small pleasant restaurant at the foot of Ness Bridge, was a good beginning. Riva's owner was delighted to serve us our first meal in Scotland. After another half hour taking pictures in the red-skyed dusk, we were more than ready for bed.

Inverness, a picturesque town of 50,900, has architecture dating back to its early beginnings as a medieval trade town. It is the administrative and trade center of the Highlands. There is much to see and do in Inverness and in the area around it, ranging from Culloden Battlefield (where Bonnie Prince Charlie saw his Jacobite troops defeated) to Cawdor Castle and Loch Ness (with the elusive "Nessie"). But our plan was a good first night's sleep, a full Scottish breakfast, and then on to the world of the North West Highlands of Scotland, the beginning of our journey of discovery.

"Grand, Wild, Savage but Most Beautiful"

Our goal was to be at Little Lodge in North Erradale in the early afternoon, a drive of seventy-five miles from east to west at the narrow waist of Scotland. Loch Maree, described by Queen Victoria as "grand, wild, savage but most beautiful," was on the way, and what a glorious introduction to the North West Highlands it was.

Ten minutes out of Inverness, across the narrow inlet of Beauly Firth, and we were in gentle green countryside where I was concentrating on driving in the left lane (wrong side) of the road. It takes at least a day to adjust from intellectual to instinctive road sense and a little longer for muscles in your left shoulder to adapt to a five-speed gearshift, also on the left.

We drove over the river Conon, past Torrachilty Wood. A sense of what was to come began with Loch Luichart and Loch Achanalt, with occasional green fields on the north side of the road. To the south, the reddish orange foothills and peaks of Sgurr Marcasaidh, Carn Garbh, and Sgurr Ghlas Leathlaid frame the lochs. The two-lane road then shifts abruptly to a winding single track with a sheer drop on the left side. This new challenge continues on for nine miles to Glen Docherty and down the glen to the small village of Kinlochewe (**Kin lohh** you).

The road from Kinlochewe follows the valley floor where the Kinlochewe River flows into Loch Maree and follows along the south side of the loch. On the far side of the loch are views of Slioch rising 3,200 feet, a stunning backdrop to the pearl-gray water. Several small islands are covered with ancient Scots Pine—reddish bark, dark green needles, and craggy shapes—surviving fragments of the Great Wood of Caledon. The trees on these islands look to have been chosen and carefully arranged by an ikebana artist whose purpose is to express the trinity of heaven, earth, and mankind. Skiffs move lazily at anchor, and in the foreground there are small patches of grass with ash and willow trees. Two newborn lambs completed the picture. A light mist softened the scene. Except for wisps of wind on the water, all was quiet. This is soul food that truly does nourish the spirit, a quality we were to find again and again in the North West Highlands.

> *And my soul spread wide its wings*
> *And flew over the still lands*
> *As if it were flying home*
> —FROM A POEM PUT TO MUSIC BY SCHUMANN

A ROYAL VIEW OF LOCH MAREE

IN *MORE LEAVES FROM the Journal of Life in the Highlands,* Queen Victoria recorded her impressions of Loch Maree on a six-day visit in September 1877. It was after publication of this book that Prime Minister Disraeli made his famous remark to the popular Queen, "we authors, ma'am."

At Loch Maree the queen and her party stayed at the Loch Maree Hotel, which is still there and not much-changed. The queen's first sight of Loch Maree was from her carriage after having bounced over the same stretch of "desolate, wild, and perfectly uninhabited country" we were to travel more than a century later.

Of her first view of Loch Maree Queen Victoria wrote, "From the top of the hill you go down a very grand pass called Glen Docherty. Here Loch Maree comes into view most beautifully . . . grand and romantic . . . the drive along the lochside for ten miles is beautiful in the extreme. The hills to the right, as you go from Kinlochewe are splendid—very high and serrated." Another day the Queen added, "The windings of the road are beautiful, and afford charming glimpses of the loch which is quite locked in by the overlapping mountains . . . here and there a fine Scotch fir, twisted, and with a stem and head like a stone-pine stands out on a rocky projection into the loch, relieved against the blue hills as in some Italian view." We discovered the scene at Loch Maree was much as it had been 125 years before.

About a day on Loch Maree the queen wrote, "It was delightful rowing through these wooded rock islands with the blue calm loch—not another sound but the oars—the lovely blue distant hills on one side and the splendid peaks of Ben Slioch and its surrounding mountains on the other." The queen had an eye for more than scenery. "Four very respectable-looking men (one a very good-looking young farmer) rowed the boat." I was reminded of art critic Alan Riding's observations on a Tate Gallery exhibition, "Exposed: The Victorian Nude." Riding wrote, "Victorians were not prudes after all, just hypocrites. . . . Even Queen Victoria, so majestically austere in public, was a party girl at heart. Please don't imagine she was thinking of England when she gave Prince Albert paintings of naked ladies as birthday presents."

The next day, after a rain, the sun came out and Queen Victoria saw "the most brilliant most complete rainbow of our life—one inside the other." This was a painting in the sky we were to share one evening at Little Lodge.

The Queen was quite taken with "my dear little sitting-room, looking on the loch. . . . The view is quite beautiful, Ben Sleach on one side, and the splendid loch, with other fine rocky mountains and green island, on the other. One would like to sketch all day." Mark Vincent, proprietor of the Loch Maree Hotel, assured me that guests can stay in the Queen Victoria Room and that the hotel has retained its style as a Victorian hunting lodge.

A Sad Test of Passion

IN HER BOOK QUEEN Victoria recounted a walk on Isle Maree
"through the tangled underwood and thicket of oak, holly and birch
. . . to the tomb of a . . . princess about whose untimely death there
is a romantic story." This is the story.

Early in the ninth century, Olaf, a handsome and headstrong
Norwegian prince and chief among Vikings, was possessed of
a deep passion for a local maiden but could not ask his beloved
to exchange "the quietude of her father's home for the restless
life of a ship of war." A wise, aged saint from the Hermitage on
Isle Maree who was said to be "of peculiar sagacity, piety, and
shrewdness" offered a solution to the disconsolate Prince Olaf.
The prince, he said, should build a tower next to the
Hermitage, making it within easy reach of the prince's galley
anchored at Poolewe on Loch Ewe and near enough the home
of the beloved's father to give him comfort.

The tower was built, the prince and his love married and all
rejoiced. "The leafy grove grew gay with joyful laughter and sweet
song." The passion of the prince and his bride and their love for
each other "grew deeper than St. Maelrubha's well." They could not
bear to be apart for even a moment. But alas, in time the prince's
men grew restless. A great campaign had been planned and duty
called. To shorten their moments apart by even a minute, Olaf
devised a plan. When his galley returned to Poolewe, his strongest
men would row the prince in his barge swiftly down the River Ewe
to Loch Maree. If all was well a white banner would show from the
barge, and if not, a black banner. The moment the prince's barge
was sighted by a lookout in the tower, the princess was to depart
Isle Maree on her barge, also flying a white or black banner.

While away in battle, the prince was sustained by a vision of
early embrace, of beginning where he and his love had left off.
But as days apart lengthened, the princess grew tormented by

doubts. Does he love war more than me? Has his passion diminished? Am I only a plaything "caressed one day and deserted the next?" Near demented, the princess planned a fateful test of Olaf's devotion. At long last the lookout announced that the prince's barge, bearing a white banner, was entering Loch Maree. The Princess departed Isle Maree in her barge, but rather than a white banner, she flew a black banner of death—to test Olaf's love. She lay on a bier covered by a white shroud with maidens grouped around pretending to weep for their departed mistress.

From a distance when the prince saw the black banner he went out of his mind. "His frenzy and wild raving grew terrible." As the barges drew abreast the prince leapt to his lost love, raised the shroud, looked in pain at her waxen face, gave a tormented agonizing cry, drew his dagger and plunged it deep into his breast. In a moment, his strong heart ceased to beat. The princess rose from her bier convinced of his passion and love, but he lay dead at her feet as if by her hand. With a pitiful cry of remorse she drew the bloody dagger from Olaf's heart and plunged it in her own.

Buried beneath sacred trees, the prince and his bride were laid with their feet toward each other, and smooth stones with carvings of medieval crosses placed over their graves.

The stones remain to this day, evidence of the sad and failed test of passion that Queen Victoria saw on her Sunday walk on Isle Maree.

Context for a Small Guest House

A THOUSAND YEARS AGO, when much of the seaboard of the North West Highlands was under Norse rule, the sheltered waters of Loch Gairloch (Lohh Gair [like hair] lohh) and nearby Loch Ewe provided safe harbor for Viking longships traveling established routes between Scandinavia, the western Highlands, and Ireland. Nothing remains of this early Norse rule except Norse place names such as Thorsdale, named after the Norse god of thunder.

Viking rule ended in 1263, when Clan MacLeod won control of the area. Violent clashes followed between the MacLeods and the rival Clan MacKenzie for the vast region. Then in 1494, as a reward for battles fought and won for King James IV, the king by Royal Charter granted Hector Roy MacKenzie (Eachainn Ruadh MacCoinnich) the lands of Gairloch and the title of First Chief.

The MacKenzies ruled this vast territory from their clan seat at Flowerdale. As with other clan chiefs in Scotland the MacKenzies had absolute power of life and death over all in their territory. This changed in the eighteenth century following a Treaty of Union that incorporated the Scottish Parliament into the Westminster Parliament to create the United Kingdom. A substantial part of the Gairloch area remains in MacKenzie ownership to this day. Land rents are paid by owners of crofts and other tenants to John MacKenzie, the seventeenth Laird of Gairloch, now occasionally in residence at Flowerdale House.

In 1850, Laird MacKenzie, who had a well-developed liking for good living, needed to increase his income. He abandoned the run-rig system by which tenants living in small groups of houses were allocated strips of land rotating each year with turns at good and bad soil. They had no incentive to improve land they were not going to farm the next year. Results were meager and rents were low. In the new crofting system, land was divided into parcels of three to five acres, with each crofter allocated a share of common grazing. These small parcels were called crofts, and crofters were allowed to build but not own their homes on them. Groups of crofts defined crofting townships whose "grazing committees" administered grazing rights, peat cutting, boundary walls, and so on. The best of the run-rig tenants were relocated to crofts, and rents went up. Selected pasture areas suitable for large flocks were not divided into crofts, but went to large-scale sheep farming, which produced another substantial source of income for the estate.

Crofts seldom, if ever, provided a living for the crofting family. To subsist, crofters also became fishermen, worked in the trades, performed services for the estate, and worked at whatever other jobs were to be had. Grazing committees still exist, as do the crofting townships along the east coast of Loch Gairloch, including North Erradale (where we stayed at Little Lodge). The forced change to crofting in the North West Highlands followed different patterns, ranging from relatively benign in the Gairloch Estate to cruel and unusual by the First Duke of Sutherland in his Assynt estates. The rights of croft tenants have changed significantly over 150 years. The nature of these changes and the forces and laws that led to them define much of what the North West Highlands has become.

A Picture of Perfection

AFTER THE SPIRITUAL HIGH of Loch Maree the day had turned dark, the painterly mist became a dull drizzle, and our body clocks let us know it was 6:00 A.M. in Boulder. With these conditions, our first view of Loch Gairloch did little to lift our spirits. A cup of soup in Gairloch and we continued on our way. A road sign just outside of Gairloch woke me up—"ELDERLY CROSSING"! While we must have gone back and forth across that point in the road a dozen times over the next three days, we never once saw an elderly.

The road narrowed to a winding, single track with a demonstrable lack of recent maintenance. Six miles on the rain stopped, the sky cleared, and we turned in to a narrow lane leading toward the loch and Little Lodge. Our first view was of this brilliant white cottage standing stoically on a heather-clad peninsula, looking over the water to the island of Skye and across to the Torridon Mountains. A small flock of sheep, several Angora goats, and a few proud hens roamed about. And there at the doorstep were Di and Inge to greet us warmly, get us to our room quickly, and invite us to a hot cup of tea and homemade biscuits.

Their dog was another matter. It was two days before Joshua accepted me and let me throw his bell-ball contraption for him to retrieve, an endless activity about which I became somewhat ambivalent.

Little Lodge is a croft house that was converted to a guesthouse with imagination and great attention to detail by its caring and cheerful proprietor-chefs, Di Johnson and Inge Ford. As croft tenants, they pay Laird MacKenzie eighteen pounds (twenty-five dollars) a year in land rent. A *Taste of Scotland* describes Little Lodge as "an idyllic retreat with superb cuisine . . . an absolutely charming experience . . . hospitality is second to none." *The Rough Guide* says, "Little Lodge is outstanding, with immaculately furnished rooms, a log-burning stove . . . and dramatic sea views as well as superb food." Both sources proved to be correct. Little Lodge was comfortable, sociable, undemanding, and in a beautiful setting, and the food was excellent. It was the right mix to continue our easy-paced adjustment to the Highlands.

Our small, attractive bedroom, one of three, was bright white with old pine wainscoting and views of the Torridon peaks. The homey sitting room was decorated with rich simplicity and arranged with the expectation that people would talk with each other—and we did, before dinner with sherry and after dinner with a dram. And yes, there was no TV at Little Lodge.

Presentation of three-course dinners was on a par with the imaginative cooking—white tablecloth, good silver, Wedgewood china, great views, and Inge's friendly service and appropriate commentary about each dish. Di was the main chef, and her kitchen garden provided most of the vegetables and herbs. Other supplies were bought daily from local sources.

The obvious question was, what were these two very civilized women doing working 24/7 in a place like this? Di Johnson was a psychotherapist with a reputation for successful parties and a limitless fund of energy, which is still very much in evidence. She is the chief cook and bottle washer and can be seen cutting grass in her spare time. Her friend Inge Ford was a school administrator. It stands to reason Inge runs the front office, deals with guest needs, and does the morning biscuits.

Di was getting tired of patients and Inge of parents, and both wanted out of the rat race in Bristol. On holiday in 1989 they learned of this crofthouse for sale, took a look at the outside (they couldn't get in but could tell it was a mess), drank in the view, and made a few inquiries. Love triumphed over reason. They made an offer and it was accepted.

It took two years to strip away an accretion of grime and bad taste; discover the covered-over fireplace (Di was whacking at a wall with a crowbar); install new plumbing, heating, and wiring; and get doors, shelves, cabinets, and all else of the right design in the right place. Workmen did most of it on their own while Di and Inge were six hundred miles away at their own jobs. Anyone who has had remodeling done knows it is hard enough to get what you want when you are right there. Calling on their experience with patients and children who needed heavy guidance, the dynamic duo came up with a brilliant show-and-tell approach to remodeling—cardboard constructions, three-dimensional models, and templates defining the size, shape, and location of what they needed.

On April 9, 1991 at 4:00 P.M. Di and Inge took a deep breath and hung out their sign at the end of the lane. At 4:30 P.M. two people showed up expecting beds and a three-course dinner. Now, after ten years, Di is still in the kitchen and eighty percent of Little Lodge guests are repeat customers.

How the Creaky Traveler Found Little Lodge

BECAUSE I LOVE PLANNING long trips I get two highs, one from planning and the other from going. My approach to planning is a nonlinear, iterative process by which each step or new piece of information may inform and modify a previous one. So once my wife and I started thinking seriously about the North West Highlands, I began to assemble a planning library, including a list of relevant Internet sites. I also checked to make sure I had the lowest-cost international calling plan. Mine was ten cents a minute to the U.K.

The Scottish Tourist Board was a great source for "where to stay" and "what to do" guides. Bookstores had relatively little on the North West Highlands because most travelers don't think beyond Skye. *Scottish Highlands and Islands: The Rough Guide* and *Scotland the Best!* were the only commercial guides worth buying. Odd notes from other guides I looked at in bookstores and the library went into my planning journal. The Internet is now clearly the best source for material on the landscape, character, and history of local areas, including photos. A good touring map is an essential tool. I began with an Ordnance Survey: Northern Scotland with the one-inch-to-four-miles scale. Once we had firmed up our route I graduated to Ordnance Survey maps at one-and-a-quarter inch to one mile.

Our ultimate decision to travel the North West Highlands was made because they looked so wild and wonderful, and not too many other travelers would be around in May. While G and I are sociable, when it comes to the outdoors we like the feeling of discovery when we have a place to ourselves. Also, even though the Highlands are deservedly famous for extraordinary walks and climbs, and for great fishing, we would be able to see and do a great deal without having to walk or climb more than we could manage. And not the least of all, when she was very young, G fell in love with a picture of Suilven (**Sool** i ven) and Canisp (**Kan** isp), two very distinctive and shapely mountains near Lochinver (Lohh **in** ver). The idea of seeing them for real was the dealmaker.

With the Highland decision made, planning our route and choosing our stopovers was the next step. Gairloch (**Gair** lohh) was a logical starting point. It was only seventy-five miles from Inverness, and Loch Maree was on the way. When it comes to where to stay, some people like to take potluck—go there and depend on serendipity. If you barrel along on a bunch of one-night stands and aren't too picky, that might work just fine. But because we were planning to stay in most places for three nights and had high expectations, we aimed for certainty. We try to apply eight criteria for our choices: (1) small, not more than six rooms; (2) distinctive personality, run by an onsite owner, not a hired hand; (3) beautifully situated; (4) ensuite room (W.C. and bath or shower), not more than one flight up, good natural light a must, view a plus; (5) opportunity to mix with other guests; (6) reputation for good food; (7) affordable price; and (8) a place where we wouldn't mind being rained in for a day.

After sorting and cross referencing source material, I came up with six or so of the best options in the area of each stopping place and made follow-up checklists: owner name, address, telephone, fax, e-mail, whether credit cards accepted, price, and source of rating or recommendation. Then I faxed or e-mailed requests for a brochure and price list, and to check availability. I also asked a question about weather or some feature. Brochures show how people present themselves, and I am always curious to see if proprietors, when they respond, add a personal note. My final step for places on the short list is a telephone call. Who sounds helpful and like someone I would like to meet?

And that is how we got to Little Lodge. Done over a period of months, this approach to planning is not that big a deal.

SETTLING IN

WE SETTLED INTO OUR room, which didn't take long because we don't really unpack. We need two off-the-ground and out-of-the-way surfaces for our roll aboard suitcases, whether luggage stands, chairs, or the tops of dressers. The other essential is to check for reading lamps on both sides of the bed and to make sure the wattage is high enough to read by. Little Lodge passed the test. For places that don't, we ask for what we need.

Next came a cup of tea with our hosts and talk about the area, meal times, and what would be for dinner. G felt it was time for a nap. I sat outside for a read and doze in the garden, with Joshua sizing me up but not yet ready to connect. After a bit, G and I went for a slow stroll up the lane, with each of us getting more used to walking with the help of a cane—and they do help. The canes, a clever folding variety, were a trip present from our daughter Emily. She had noticed more and more listing as G favored her right hip and I my right knee. With two rights we were able to synchronize cane and step movements and march proudly together. Canes have another great advantage. They are a symbol of need, and others tend to add a little something in their kindly treatment of you.

The scenery around Little Lodge is comfortable and not challenging, with a scattering of white croft houses in the distance, a few lambs and their unexcitable mothers, the peaks of the Torridons to the south, and the beginning edge of the Atlantic to the west—all our constant companions. It is perfect for two people on their first full day in Scotland and barely out of first gear.

When we got back, Brenda and Jeff Gordon had arrived from Lincolnshire on their eighth visit to Little Lodge. They were, like us, of an age when "the war" is always World War II. Jeff trained bomber navigators, and Brenda was in the British equivalent of the WACS. G had been in London through the blitz and the rest of the war drafting huge "double elephant" sized engineering drawings of welding tools used to repair damaged ship hulls underwater. Brenda also shared G's enthusiasm for word puzzles, especially one called Codewords that quite naturally has no word clues but some complex number/letter linkage. It's beyond me. After dinner Di and Inge joined us, and conversation turned to rhymes and limericks. G's contribution won going away.

> As I was walking on the heath
> I met a man with many teeth
> He showed them to me one by one
> I thought that was a lot of fun

MORE MEANDERING

BREAKFAST! HAVING HAD A fine dinner, a comfortable night, and a wake-up cup of tea in our room (once I figured out where to plug in the pot cord—you get on your knees and hunt behind the small bookcase), neither G nor I were prepared for what came next. Choose any or all of the following: juice, porridge, dry cereal, yogurt, fresh fruit salad, smoked haddock, kippers, smoked salmon, bacon, sausage, haggis, blood pudding, cooked tomato, eggs (any way you like), oat-cakes, muffins, and cold toast, all manner of homemade preserves, tea, coffee, and hot chocolate. The cold toast is one of the miracles of U.K. cuisine. Toast is always (always) served cold, slices cut diagonally, six pieces lined up vertically in a silver rack like good soldiers. Pay anything. Go anywhere. It's always the same—cold, diagonal, lined up, silver rack. Go figure.

The critical thing after breakfast is to go somewhere or move around, or you will be back asleep in no time. The idea of lunch after a giant breakfast is beyond belief. It was this way for the entire trip. Maybe coffee or tea, a biscuit or two, a banana or an orange, but that was it until dinner, except possibly for a dram.

We decided to head for Badachro (**Bat** a hhrow [like crow]), a protected bay on the south shore of Loch Gairloch. The publican at the Badachro Inn talked about changes in Badachro. From a fishing and cod processing center that yielded cash for many crofters and their wives, and sent barrel after barrel of salted cod off to Spain, it had now become an upscale place of high-priced summer and retirement homes for wealthy "incomers." The harbor had also become a preferred destination for visiting yachts.

Being the only pub around, the inn remained the place where locals came for a dram. I asked him if alcoholism was a problem. "Not at all," he said. "Without alcoholics we would go broke."

"Does it lead to crime or other problems?" I asked.

"No, just a lot of single car accidents when they drive off the road into a ditch and we have to get them and their car home."

This sanguine view is certainly not universal. A notice in the *Gairloch & District Times* on May 4, 2001, under the heading "HELP LINES," read "Al-Anon & Alateen for families and friends of problem drinkers. Meetings in this area are held regularly." But then there are no Alcoholics Anonymous (AA) groups anywhere in the area. So, it would seem that while families and friends suffer, the drinkers feel no pain.

It would appear Robert Burns' observations in "Scotch Drink," written in 1785, are still apt.

> *Gie him strong drink until he wink,*
> *That's sinking in despair;*
> *An' liquor guid to fire his bluid,*
> *That's prest wi' grief and care:*
> *There let him bouse, an' deep carouse,*
> *Wi' bumpers flowing o'er,*
> *Till he forgets his loves or debts,*
> *An' minds his griefs no more.*

TWO-AND-A-HALF BILLION YEARS (BP)

THE DRIVE FROM GAIRLOCH to Poolewe (**Pool** yoo) is five miles. Just out of Gairloch the road rises steeply from sea level to a moorland plateau and passes close to Loch Tollaidh before dropping abruptly again to sea level at Poolewe. A thoughtfully placed viewpoint on the plateau offered us a long view of this "boggy, rocky, mountainous land" and a lesson in what geologists call a "spectacular tectonic happening." We could see the small settlements that were restricted to the relatively few fertile pockets scattered along the coast and along the bottom of narrow glens (valleys) that wound inland from the fjord-like sea lochs. Freshwater lochs (lakes) of all sizes were scattered across the landscape.

We were looking at the force of the ice age, some two million years of "plucking and grinding," and, after the big melt, an added ten thousand years of weathering—the erosive power of wind, water, freeze, and thaw over time. As glaciers advanced, huge rocks imbedded in them smoothed and polished surfaces and gouged armchairs ("corries," semicircular basins) in valley heads. Melt water off the hills created lochs in the corries. Retreating glaciers also deposited soil and rocks of infinite size and shape, creating hummocks and other surface forms and textures. The spectacular peaks we saw on our journey—Suilven, Canisp, Ben More, Stac Pollaidh—are the surviving remnants of sedimentary rock, Torridonian sandstone. Silver-colored topping like a dusting of snow is Cambrian quartzite. Highlanders are very proud of their ancient rocks, especially the Lewision gneiss, dated 2.5 billion years before present (B.P.), that underlies much of northwest Scotland. This is a geologist's paradise.

POINT COUNTERPOINT—LAMBS AND CONVOYS

POOLEWE SITS PLACIDLY AT the head of Loch Ewe where the River Ewe connects Loch Maree, a freshwater loch, and Loch Ewe, a sheltered sea loch. Aside from its natural beauty, the River Ewe has the distinction of being the shortest river in Scotland, a little over five thousand feet. Water tumbling from it forms a small bay with a few pleasant whitewashed cottages and the centuries old Pool House Hotel around it. Not too many years ago the bay was an active port for boats to the Outer Isles. Much earlier it was a calm harbor for Viking longships because, unlike other west coast lochs, Loch Ewe faces north, protecting it from harsh westerly winds.

As we drove north out of Poolewe along the east shore of the Cove Peninsula, the narrow, single-track road rose above Loch Ewe. We could see almost all the hills to the northwest and the scattered crofting communities clinging to land beside the sea. The countryside around us was harsh and unforgiving. Then, as if superimposed on this challenging landscape, a fertile pocket—a big bright green pasture—swept up from the road and down again to the loch. The pasture was dotted with pure white lambs born not more than the day before, all lying quietly at the feet of their placid mothers. In the next field young lambs bounced around as if on four pogo sticks. When they nurse, their heads tuck under, their rumps stick up, and their little tails wag in furious delight. This was a sight we could never get enough of.

In counterpoint, just beyond this bucolic scene, the Russian Convoy Club's simple stone memorial, etched with these words to shipmates lost, stood at the entrance to Lock Ewe.

> *In Memory of Our Shipmates*
> *Who Sailed from Loch Ewe*
> *During World War II*
> *They Lost Their Lives*
> *In the Bitter Arctic Sea Battles*
> *In North Russia*
> *And Never Returned*
> *To This Tranquil Anchorage*
> *We Will Always Remember Them*

Loch Ewe was a World War II assembly base for convoys that moved desperately needed arms 1,600 miles through the Barents Sea and White Sea to the Russian supply ports of Archangel and Murmansk. An entry from one ship's log reads, "Air battles on again. All driven away. Battling is furious. Fog banks save the day. Convoy fighting ice, mines, bombs, torpedoes, and subs." Other entries speak of "freezing spray, blinding snow, driving sleet, and storms," some storms so violent that they tore apart welded seams in hulls and broke older merchant ships apart.

Forty convoys totaling nearly eight hundred ships moved 375,000 trucks, 22,000 aircraft, and millions of shoes, rifles, ammunition, and whatever. The loss rate was high, especially early in the war. Of the thirty-three departing ships in Convoy #17, seventeen survived. Twenty of the thirty-three departing ships in Convoy #18 survived.

Now, after nearly sixty years, lighter memories mix with the melancholy. Older residents of the Loch Ewe community talk about the "loch being black with ships, when you could walk from one side to the other without getting your feet wet." Between merchant seamen, military personnel, and a "let's live it up now attitude," there were a lot of parties, dances, and high times in Poolewe.

THE AROMA OF HAPPINESS

G AND I STILL smile when we think of Connie and Michael Inman in their Bridge Coffee Shop & Cottage Gallery in Poolewe because they were so wonderfully happy. They glowed. They had this cheering aroma that has stayed with us. Hard to imagine, but real.

Coming back from the Cove Peninsula, we stopped at this whitewashed cottage for a cup of coffee. Inside were five small tables, with everything bright and sparkling, the counter full of cakes, scones and behind the small counter, Connie and Michael with welcoming smiles. We learned that they came from Leeds, an industrial town in the Midlands. Michael left high school at seventeen and went to work in a record shop, then at an insurance company. There, after twenty-seven years, he worked his way up to financial advisor. Connie told us she left school at fifteen and went to work for a clothing manufacturer as a junior sales assistant. After thirty-three years she had risen to sales manager and then was declared redundant. Thank you. Goodbye.

Completing each other's sentences, Connie and Michael told us they had been coming to the Highlands on vacation for ten years with a growing dream of working for themselves and a better quality of life. The redundancy bit did it. And here they were running a coffee shop and art gallery in Poolewe. Michael asked us to sample each of the goodies he starts baking at 4:00 every morning. Connie does the soup and doubles between the coffee shop and gallery/gift shop. They are very pleased with themselves. Connie summed it up: "Now we can be who we are."

Two Feet Tall and Ready for Battle

WHO WOULD HAVE THOUGHT a couple of dolls with an attitude could get to us? In another whitewashed cottage, there they were, two feet tall, with dagger and broadsword ready for battle—chiefs of the Buchanan, Campbell, Macdonald, Mackay, Mackenzie, Macleod, and Macdona clans. These extraordinary and accurate seventeenth-century clan dolls are the creation of Mary Buchanan, one-time schoolteacher and clothing manufacturer.

Mary took us through her garden to a neat and precisely organized pottery where she sculpts, casts, fires, and hand paints the different doll heads and faces of each clan in editions of thirty dolls. In a workshop next to the pottery, Mary cuts and sews precisely detailed clothing for each clan. A year of research and planning is evident in every detail—oak buttons, hand spun bonnet, dirk (dagger) and broadsword made by a Scotch armorer, long linen shirt with buttoned cuffs, woolen jacket, tartan plaid dyed and woven to doll scale for each clan, and natural hair for flowing locks and fierce beard. At full size the plaid is sixty inches wide and twelve to eighteen feet long. Clansmen first pleated and then wrapped the plaid around their bodies by laying the plaid on the ground, lying on top of it, and then fastening the two unpleated ends with a belt.

Mary is a keen, alert, intense woman, and it seemed to me that it was her dash and spirit that made the extraordinarily crafted and realistic dolls come alive. Mary talked about having started out teaching home economics (cooking and dressmaking) in Glasgow for five years. She and husband Jim, a science teacher, wanted out of Glasgow for a better life in the North West Highlands, where they had walked and climbed for many years. Jim was offered a science teaching post at the Gairloch High School, and twenty years ago their new life began.

Having no job, Mary had a chance to try out a business idea that grew out of their walking and climbing—handmade high performance clothing for arduous conditions. That was the beginning of Slioch, her one-woman business—design, cut, sew, promote, sell, deliver. Royal Air Force mountain rescue teams were early adopters of

the clothing, and after twenty successful years Mary sold a flourish-
ing business. But dolls? She explained, "I wanted to create another
business where I could work on my own (being able to go for a walk
or garden when the sun shone—very important in this part of the
world). I also wanted to make something of value that required many
of my skills, so the idea for the dolls just came about."

At a thousand dollars each, the dolls are not child's play.

INCOMERS AND CROFTERS

DI AND INGE CAME from Bristol, Connie and Michael from Leeds,
and Mary and Jim from Glasgow. All are "incomers," people who
move in from somewhere else. They came to the North West
Highlands for a better life, not to be rich and famous. These small "e"
entrepreneurs worked hard and took risks, and in the process, began
adding to the local economies with new business and jobs for locals,
the folk with crofting roots. There are subtle distinctions, such as
being "real local" versus becoming local by "marrying in" or "mucking
in"—which means working hard, not putting on airs and pitching in.

Crofters provide continuity in the character and cooperative noncompetitive style of life in the small crofting townships and villages.
While they live on crofts and are adept at obtaining croft subsidies,
few locals if any depend on agriculture to survive. They supplement
croft income as they always have with other work -- county roads,
driving the school bus, music teacher, store clerk, carpenter, fishing
guide. The incomers bring new resources, new energy and new ideas.

Back we drove—another wondrous look Loch Maree, then over
the high moor, along Loch Gairloch, and to the comfort of Little
Lodge. After another easy evening, and the next morning a more than
you can eat breakfast, we enjoyed a leisurely departure. It was overcast, but cheery Di and Inge, the ever-hopeful Joshua, and even a few
curious sheep came to wish us well and on our way.

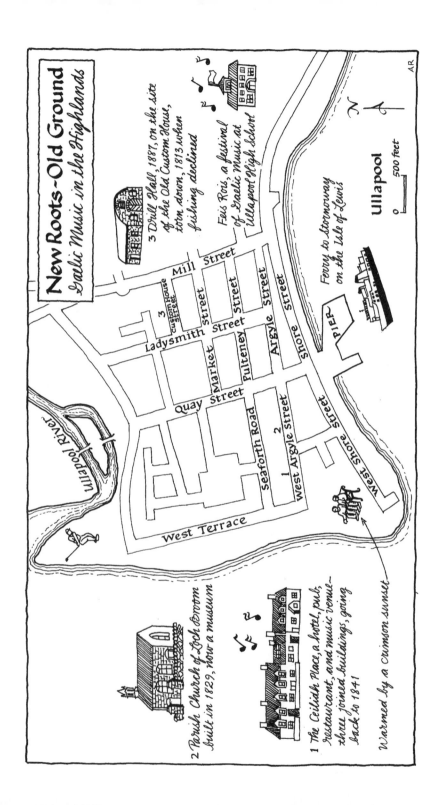

New Roots~Old Ground
Gaelic Music in the Highlands

3 Drill Hall, 1887, on the site of the Old Custom House, torn down, 1813 when fishing declined

Fèis Rois, a festival of Gaelic music at Ullapool High School

Ullapool

0   500 feet

AR

Mill Street

Custom House Street

3

Ladysmith Street

Market Street

Pulteney Street

Argyle Street

Shore Street

Quay Street

Seaforth Road

2

West Argyle Street

1

West Terrace

West Shore Street

PIER

Ferry to Stornoway on the Isle of Lewis

Ullapool River

2 Parish Church of Loch Broom built in 1829, now a museum

1 The Ceilidh Place, a hotel, pub, restaurant, and music venue— three joined buildings, going back to 1841

Warmed by a crimson sunset

CHAPTER THREE

ULLAPOOL, FEIS ROIS, AND THE CEILIDH

ULLAPOOL AND THE UNFAITHFUL RED HERRING

WE HEADED NORTH TO our next stop at Ullapool (Ul la pool) where we had been invited to sit in on Feis Rois (Faysh Rawsh), a tuition (teaching) festival of traditional Gaelic music and song. Also, it would be a chance to talk with Jean Urquhart, Scottish National Party parliamentary candidate and owner of The Ceilidh Place, a hotel cum cultural center.

It was a gloomy "we should have stayed in bed" kind of day. I drove. G dozed. A supposed "classic view" of the Anteallach peaks was completely hidden by clouds. And we gave a pass to the famous 164-foot Falls of Measach that plunge dramatically into the mile-long Corrieshalloch Gorge. (We are not afflicted by "travelers' remorse," a form of torment many tourists have when they miss something on their checklist.)

The big event of the morning was our stop for petrol. The price translated into six dollars per U.S. gallon and made me appreciate the twenty-seven miles per gallon our car was getting. The final section of the highway to Ullapool followed the route of the "Destitution Road," one of a number of such roads built during the famines of the 1800s to provide survival jobs for local people. The road crested a final hill, and there on Loch Broom was Ullapool.

Most of the country we had traveled up to that point—Loch

Maree, Gairloch, Loch Ewe, Poolewe—was of nature's own design. Roads followed natural contours. Cottages and villages had an organic feel. And here was Ullapool, an engineers dream, a perfect grid of straight streets with neat rows of white cottages all built to the same set of specifications, planned and paid for in the late 1800s by the British Fisheries Society. And the red herring was the reason.

The Highland Society of London, a group of "noblemen and gentlemen" who were not averse to improving their fortunes, was founded in 1778, one of their goals being to give "practical encouragement to fisheries in the Highlands." In 1786 they launched The British Society for Extending the Fisheries and Improving the Sea Coasts of the Kingdom, which fortunately came to be known as the British Fisheries Society. The society saw profit and virtue marching side by side as they began their search in 1787 for the location of a fishing village. The village would, they said, promote employment and encourage inhabitants in "the love of labour and good order [in a] new framework for human life in the countryside." Nowhere did they consider this more necessary "than on the shores of the west Highlands."

Moving quickly, in 1787 the Society purchased a thousand acres of land from Lord MacLeod, including fifty-seven arable acres that had been farmed and seventy-four acres suitable only for pasture. In June the sloop Gilmerton arrived with eight thousand bricks and 1,967 pieces of timber and other goods, along with fifteen workmen, thirty-nine wives and children, and one fisherman. Work began on the fishing village of Ullapool according to the grid plan and building specifications of surveyor David Aitkens. An early priority was "a suitable schoolhouse to answer occasionally for a chapel."

By 1790 Ullapool consisted of eighteen buildings. Commercial buildings were lined up on Shore Street facing the new breakwater and pier—the Red Herring House, a shed in which to dry nets, shops for a boat builder and a cooper, a storehouse for salt, and another storehouse for casks. On Argyle, the next street up, ten small cottages stood in a row, and then on Seaforth Road were the schoolhouse/chapel and the schoolmaster's house. With the basics in place, the

British Fisheries Society was ready to attract settlers who would fish.

The society understood the herring was a "shifting ambulatory fish" and reasoned that the settlers had to have enough land to survive by growing food in a bad fishing season. But on the other hand, and here was the cynical kicker, "the Highlander was thought to prefer a low standard of living to hard work and if he was to fish at all he must not have enough land to live on entirely." Lease terms offered to settlers reflected this view. On a neat grid of streets, a settler could obtain a ninety-nine-year lease for a sixty-foot-wide lot on which to build a white cottage, with stables and outhouse behind at an annual rent of five pounds. With this the settler could also lease half an acre of farmland at five shillings a year for five years and up to five acres of undeveloped land at one shilling an acre for ten years. In addition, on the society's land, the settler could pasture two cows in summer, dig peat and take stone and sand "freely for his own use."

By 1878 there were more than forty cottages. The fishing fleet included thirty small fishing boats belonging to settlers and three vessels of twenty to seventy tons each owned by Ullapool. "When the shoals of Herrings come to the neighborhood the whole inhabitants of the village may be considered fishermen or fish curers . . . all that can be spared from necessary occupations . . . come down to partake of the profits of the Herring Fishery." But alas, this was the exception. The Gaelic sage who opined, "The mines of the sea are yearly renewed," was, in a word, dead wrong. The faithless red herring decided they liked the east coast better, and at the same time the world market for salt herring declined.

After several poor seasons Ullapool ceased being ready for the odd times when shoals of herring did come to Loch Broom. Nets, barrels, and salt were not readily available. Boats were not seaworthy. "Ullapool gradually sank from its hopeful beginnings and in the first half of the nineteenth century there was little work and much hardship there." In 1847 the British Fisheries Society gave up the ghost and sold Ullapool and all its land leases to Sir James Mathieson for five thousand pounds. It was a hundred years before Ullapool prospered again.

Shoals of tourists are Ullapool's new catch. Gift shops, pubs, and bed-and-breakfasts have replaced the net drying shed and salt storehouse. There is even a private launch to take high rollers to Altnaharrie Inn for $110 two-star Michelin dinners, where they can spend up to $600 per person for meals and a room. The daily ferry to Stornaway on the Island of Lewis moved from Poolewe to Ullapool in the mid 1950s, with its coming and going punctuating each day. Trips to view seabird colonies, dolphins, and porpoises in the Summer Isles are hawked from kiosks all along Ullapool's shingle beach. Long distance fishing fleets, including factory mother ships and crews from all over Europe, have discovered Ullapool as a safe anchorage and a good shipping point for refrigerator trucks. But still, at the heart of prosperous Ullapool, there is the old town, with its white cottages set out in neat rows along the street grid laid out more than two hundred years ago.

THE FEISEAN MOVEMENT—NEW ROOTS IN OLD GROUND

ULLAPOOL HIGH SCHOOL STANDS in sharp contrast to the old town. It is a modern yellow brick building of universal design. As G and I walked in, I wondered why the architecture of most school buildings expresses so little of their educational purpose or the community they serve. During the week 212 students from Ullapool and crofting townships in the area fill the space. On this weekend two hundred men and women were creating a joyful festival of Gaelic music and song at the Feis Rois Inbhich.

This was the 11th Adult Feis (festival)—three full days of master classes and workshops of traditional music, song, and dance; Gaelic conversation classes; evenings full of ceilidhs (talk and entertainment); dancing; and sessions (informal music groups). I found Feis Rois when I was planning the trip and asked www.google.com about "Gaelic Music in the North West Highlands." Feis Rois (Festival Ross) popped up on www.musicscotland.com/feisrois. I called the feis office in

Scotland and lucked out when Rita Hunter, the engaging and encouraging manager, answered. Serendipity prevailed. The annual adult feis was scheduled in early May, Rita invited us to sit in, and there we were.

The halls of Ullapool High School rang with the sound of music from every classroom—fiddle (fidheall), flute (duiseal), Gaelic song (seinn orain gaidhlig), guitar (giotar), wire harp (clarsach), pipes (piob), tin whistle (feadag), step dancing (dannsa ceum), and boisterous group work (comhlan) when musicians put it all together. The tutors were top-of-the-line professional performers, including Gaelic singer Christine Primrose, harpist Alison Kinnaird, and fiddler Aonghas Grant. The students were young adults, most in their twenties and thirties, serious about their music and having a wonderful time. Many were music teachers or heading in that direction.

We spent the evening at The Ceilidh Place where informal groups jammed into every corner were playing away for the sheer joy of it. There was no lack of the odd dram or draft about. As we talked it was clear these young adults found great pleasure and comradeship playing with others "who feel as I do." While the pleasure of creating music makes for a pretty good high, it was clear that something deeper was involved. Playing tin whistles and fiddles and guitars, these men and women talked about a "personal connection to Celtic roots" and being part of a "significant and growing cultural development." One young man confessed, "Before I got involved in this music scene my only connection to the MacLeod clan was a tartan sweater my mother gave me when I was twelve. This [music] makes me feel connected, and I want to share it with my own kids and their friends."

Folk music in Scotland followed the Joan Baez and Ewan McColl pattern of the 1950s focusing on traditional ballads. In 1978 Runrig, a ceilidh group in the Highlands, broke through with original music and a traditional sound in Gaelic that appealed to teenagers on up. This led to a number of "Gaelic roots bands" playing traditional and new Gaelic music, helping set the stage for the feisean movement.

In a formal sense, the feisean movement began on the small remote Outer Hebrides island of Barra, nearly four hours from Oban.

Barra is four miles wide and eight miles long with glacial mountains, prehistoric ruins, sandy beaches, and a predominantly Catholic population of 1,300 (who are said to be "laid-back and welcoming"). In 1981, Father Colin MacInnes, a Catholic priest, and Dr. Angus MacDonald, a prize-winning piper, were having a dram and bemoaning the fact that the Gaelic language and culture were not being passed on to young people. The idea of a feis was born. With communication being easy on Barra and the idea proving popular (there are not a lot of distractions on Barra), the island-wide festival happened. Singing, dancing, drama, and traditional music spilled out of performance halls and into the streets with improv groups all over the place. This success in 1981 evolved into a giant annual two-week event that attracted performers and participants from all over the Highlands and islands.

In 1986, Christine Martin, a music teacher on Barra, told a mainland friend, Kate Martin, about the remarkable cultural impact the feis was having on Barra's young and old. Martin, who was connected with the Highland Council Community Education Service, promoted the idea for a feis for young people in Ross and Cromarty, and Feis Rois was born with its first feis held in Ullapool for kids up to age seventeen. Feis Rois was adopted by the Ross and Cromarty District Council and now has three divisions: Oigridh, ages eight through twelve; nan Deugair, ages twelve through eighteen; and Inbhich, adult.

The Island of Skye held its first feis in 1990, and the movement took off all over the Highlands. The feisean movement has now spread to thirty communities and involves more than 3,500 young people in summer and holiday tuition festivals of the Gaelic arts. There are also over 1,300 classes year-round. An instrument "bank" lends fiddles, flutes, and other instruments to kids just starting out.

I asked Rita to explain the feis growth and its self-sustaining quality. She offered a string of reasons: participation and performance is noncompetitive, so everyone wins; self-taught but wonderfully skilled older people provide a large pool of local tutors who love teaching kids and bask in their admiration; there is an outward spiral—students become tutors, who reach more students, who produce more tutors, who reach more students; word-of-mouth; grass roots community ownership and support; and an economic spin-off as the feisian movement grows and produces career opportunities for teachers and professional musicians. It occurred to me that Rita—a prize-winning singer at Scottish song competitions, a BBC presenter of traditional music, and a festival organizer—should add herself to the list of the primary reasons for success of the feisian movement.

Feis Rois made another significant contribution to the quality of our trip. At the end of the day, Christine Primrose hauled out a huge batch of tapes. After intensive consultation, G emerged with six of them. Our rental car had a tape deck, and throughout the rest of our trip we were able to listen to all manner of Gaelic music that spoke meaningfully of the country we traveled. We didn't need to understand the words to grasp the feeling of haunting songs like "Cuir culaibh ri Assainte" (Turning Your Back on Assynt).

Cuir culaibh cuir culaibh
    Turning your back, turning your back
Cuir culaibh ri Assainte
    Turning your back on Assynt
Cuir cul ri tir nan Gaidheal
    Turning your back on the land of the Highlander
Far 'n robh mi og is amaideach
    Where I was young and foolish
Ach duil gu 'n till mi dhachaidh ann
    But I hope to return there

DOING THE CEILIDH

WHEN DI JOHNSON AT Little Lodge learned we were headed to Ullapool for the Feis Rois, she told me I really had to talk with Jean Urquhart, who ran The Ceilidh (kay-lee) Place hotel and was also

standing (running) for a seat in Parliament. As it turned out, calling The
Ceilidh Place a hotel is rather like saying the Queen Elizabeth is a boat.

On a quiet evening, G and I ambled up from Shore Street to West
Argyle, turned left past the post office and the museum, and walked
into a storm of traditional music. There were informal groups (sessions) making music at full blast all over the place—four fiddlers fid-
dling in one corner of the pub bar, three young beauties tootling on
tin whistles in another corner, a guitar duo center stage, Gaelic
singing in the parlor, and upstairs a wire harp trio producing the
music of angels. It was Feis Rois weekend and the place was rocking.
Jean was behind the bar pulling a pint of Guinness and said we should
meet later in the evening when things might be a bit quieter and have
a dram and a visit. (When we hooked up again the next day she was
helping out in the coffee shop—she was clearly a hands-on manager.)

From listening to her it is clear The Ceilidh Place is a deeply personal expression of Jean and her late husband Robert, a well-known
actor whose Scottish roots were of the ancient Urquhart clan. His
distinguished career spanned more than forty years of stage, cinema,
and television roles. I confess to a special, however distant, connection with Robert Urquhart, because he appeared in *The Avengers*, a television series with Diana Rigg playing the cool and superbly able
Mrs. Emma Peel. Robert and Jean started The Ceilidh Place in 1970
in an old boatshed attached to the Urquhart family home in Ullapool.
According to Jean, they served "modest refreshments and generous
helpings of entertainment." In Robert's words:

> *Eating and meeting*
> *Talking and singing*
> *Such is the ceilidh*
> *The joy of my life*

Ceilidh is Gaelic for "visit." It came to mean informal, extemporane-
ous entertainments Highlanders provided for each other—music, song,
poetry, dance, and good talk along with the odd dram, frequently of the

Mason jar variety. The joy of the ceilidh Robert and Jean shared with others fueled the growth of The Ceilidh Place. To provide more space, they added the Urquhart home and then the house next door. Altogether The Ceilidh Place is a wonderfully eclectic collection of spaces that call for ceilidh—two parlors, a pub type bar, performance space, exhibition room, bookstore, coffee shop, and restaurant. And incidentally, there are thirteen hotel rooms and bunkhouse space for thirty-three. The hotel had an auspicious beginning. The first guest, a woman from New York, showed up with her companion—a chair-sized teddy bear who sat opposite her at dinner.

Now, most nights the public rooms of The Ceilidh Place are filled with conversation, music, and other happenings. There are also a variety of scheduled performances. One month, for example, these ranged from the Scottish Guitar Quintet and a piping recital to the All Stars of Jazz. Jean said that probably the biggest success and most meaningful to her "was a group of young traditional musicians, Ceilidh Trail, ten young folk with an overabundance of talent playing their way around the Highlands and giving concerts every night. The great thing is that the music scene is getting better and better all the time. More and more people are beginning to play for enjoyment, and it is taking its place again in our culture." It is especially interesting to see the merger of traditional and popular cultures, with one the point of departure for the other. According to Jean, the scene is "moving on, not all old and staid. One young band, Croft No. Five, have just made their first CD, and they have taken old Gaelic airs to new and dizzy heights."

Jean insists The Ceilidh Place runs itself, giving her time to be a Director of the University of Highlands Project, Vice-Chairman (not chairperson) of the Eden Court Theatre Board in Inverness, Chairman of the Scottish Booksellers Association, Director of Feis Rois, and spokesman for the Scottish Federation of Small Business. And when we talked, Jean was also the Scottish National Party (SNP) candidate for the Ross, Skye, and Inverness West seat in the Westminster (UK) Parliament.

As it turned out, Jean did not win the election. It was certainly not for lack of intensity or passion for the Scottish cause. The political scene was in transition, and this may have been a factor. For years the goal of the SNP had been a Scotland independent of England, as it was until 1707. It was then that the Treaty of Union incorporated the Scottish Parliament into the Westminster Parliament in London, establishing the United Kingdom. Many Scots opposed the move passionately at the time, and for nearly three hundred years thereafter.

Now with devolution, a degree of control over their own destiny has returned to the Scots. The political instrument is the new Scottish Parliament sitting in Edinburgh. It was elected in 1999, achieving "independence" within the framework of the United Kingdom— England, Wales, Northern Ireland, and Scotland. The Scottish Parliament and its Executive are now responsible for health, education, economic development, transport, law and home affairs, the environment, agriculture and fisheries, sports, and arts. Parliament in Westminster, governing the U.K., now includes seventy-two Scottish seats (of 659 total) and retains control of defense, foreign affairs, and fiscal policy, including budget. The SNP now has five of the seventy-two Westminster seats, down from eleven several elections back. As a result of devolution, the total number of Scottish seats will be reduced to fifty-nine at the next election.

In the Scottish Parliament the SNP, with thirty-five of 129 seats (twenty-seven percent), is the official opposition to a coalition government of Labour (fifty-six seats) and Liberal Democrat (seventeen seats). With devolution a fact, the SNP manifesto has shifted the party position from "freedom now" to looking "forward to the day when the people of Scotland will be ready to move forward to independence and full membership in the European Union."

Where devolution will take Scotland and the political future of Jean Urquhart and the SNP are beyond the ken of the Creaky Traveler. However, one thing is sure. Whatever happens, the women of Scotland will have a strong say in it. Women total 37.2 percent of the members of the Scottish Parliament, the third-highest proportion in European federal parliaments, led only by Sweden's at 42.7 percent and Denmark's at 37.4 percent. Women in the U.K. Parliament log in at only 18.6 percent, and women in the U.S. Congress log in at a dismal 13.8 percent between Spain (14.9 percent) and Ireland (13.3 percent). France comes in last with 5.6 percent. While we are on the subject of women in Scotland, it is interesting to note that Scottish law made desertion grounds for divorce in 1573. England didn't get around to this for another 364 years, in 1937.

THE TOURIST THING

ON OUR LAST EVENING in Ullapool we took a pleasant tourist stroll down Shore Street, dropping in at a music store for another Gaelic tape, checking out the woolens in another store, having a pint at the Ferry Boat Inn (known locally as the FBI), and then watching the arrival of the Stornaway ferry as it came into the pier just across from the FBI. I always find it a good game to watch the arrival process, with the ferry maneuvering into position, hawsers thrown and tied, gangplank let down, and then a wonderful array of people coming off, and G and I speculating on who they are and where they are going.

As in all good endings, there was a glorious crimson sunset.

The next day our lives would find a new dimension when we entered the Coigach Peninsula and discovered a small world apart.

CHAPTER FOUR

COIGACH PENINSULA

A SMALL WORLD APART

WELCOME TO THE COIGACH (**koik** ohh) Peninsula, rural and isolated, five miles wide and twelve miles long, spread out over a rocky, windswept slope of hills. Whitewashed cottages string out in low-lying pockets along the shore of Loch Broom, with the Summer Isles silhouetted against the Hebrides in the distance. Only 261 men, women, and children live in the crofting townships of Coigach—Reiff, Blairbuie, Altandhu, Polbain, Meml, Achiltibuie, Polglass, Bandenscallie, Acheninver, Achduart, and Achnahaird.

For the people of the Coigach Peninsula:
- The bank comes every Friday.
- The doctor from Ullapool holds "surgery" each Wednesday morning and brings his portable pharmacist's dispensary.
- Angus MacLeod runs a twice-daily minibus twenty-five miles to Ullapool.
- In term time MacLeod's bus doubles as the school bus for the twenty-two Coigach kids in grades eight through thirteen who go to Ullapool High School, traveling an hour each way.
- Primary school in Achiltibuie has seventeen kids in one classroom, grades one through four; and ten in the other classroom, grades

five through seven. Traveling music, phys. ed., and Gaelic language teachers come once a week.

- The public library rolls in on Wednesdays. Coffee and tea are available in the morning.
- A hairdresser opens shop once a month, by appointment.
- The small general store in Polbain stocks twenty-five brands of Scotch.
- Hector MacKenzie has a workshop and can repair most things that go wrong with a car or other machinery.

Coigach has two bars, a small upscale hotel, a couple of B&Bs, several self-catering cottages for let, a post office, the primary school, and a bagpipe school of some note. There is also a new £615,000 (about $1 million) community center that took thirteen years of fundraising and community dedication to build. The main hall holds two hundred people, about two-thirds of the peninsula's population, and with its great acoustics, has become a premier venue for music groups from all over Scotland. You can ceilidh at the center most Fridays.

Coigach was one of the last peasant, preindustrial enclaves in Scotland. The isolation and rural character of Coigach remain, but its crofts have changed. At best only a few vegetables are grown for family consumption, and fewer than ten percent of the crofts run any significant number of sheep. Most work is in fish farming, construction, roadwork, driving the school bus, and the tourist trade. While there is little nostalgia for some lost age of Celtic innocence, the traditional nineteenth-century land holding pattern of crofting persists. This may be what accounts for the cooperative and noncompetitive character of the Coigach community. Mutual help seems to come naturally. The community center is an example. No one in Coigach makes a lot of money or is very poor, and there seems to be a high level of contentment.

One thing in particular struck me about the social and economic character of Coigach. While there are few apparent "us and them" distinctions among people based on class, lifestyle, housing, or religion, one clear line is drawn—local versus incomer—with some fine shadings in-between. In 1989, Angus MacLeod made a study of the local/incomer status of all 261 Coigach residents. He found forty percent of the residents were "local," and sixty percent were "incomers." Of the incomers, nearly half had come to Coigach in the period between 1980 and 1989, and their ages were about the same as the "receiving population." So, as in Gairloch and Poolewe, the bulk of the incomers were the Dis and Inges and Michaels and Connies who came to make a new life for themselves. They "mucked in," bringing fresh energy to a traditional community.

These are MacLeod's numbers of local/incomer distribution.

Born and Bred Locals

with one local parent	60
with two local parents	10
parent not local—born	
local of incomers	35
Total "Local"	105

Incomers

Scottish	85
English	67
Other	04
Total Incomers	156
Total Population	261

Then there is the issue of "white settlers." Of the 105 homes in Coigach, locals occupy fifty-four, and incomers occupy the other fifty-one. Of the fifty-one incomer homes, thirty are owned and twenty-one either rented or come with the job, such as fish farming. But here's the rub. In addition to 105 homes occupied by Coigach residents, there are another eighty-two classified as "holiday homes." Those that are owned by Coigach families are ordinarily let to tourists, providing employment and income. The other holiday homes are seen as "havens" for the wealthy who come from the Scottish lowlands and England and occupy their holiday homes for only a few weeks a year.

They contribute little to Coigach economic and social life. We found these homes easy enough to identify by signs of gentrification and a convertible Jaguar sitting out front. These people, we were told, are not "ordinary folk" but (pause for sneer) "white settlers."

I learned that while incomers cannot gain entry to the exclusive club of locals, there are few if any social or community activities or jobs to which entry is denied. After a number of informal chats and a few drams with locals and incomers, it became clear that there is far from universal agreement on who fits where on the local-incomer-white settler spectrum. I therefore decided to make my own contribution to the debate and reader edification by creating a "real real local" to "white settler" scale. It ranges from plus 200 to minus 200.

Classification	Scale
Real Real Local: 2 Local Parents	+200
Real Local: 1 Local Parent	150
Born Local To Incomer	100
Incomer Married to Local, Neighborly and Mucks In	75
Incomer, Neighborly and Mucks In	50
Incomer, Not Objectionable But Not Much More	0
Incomer, Not Likeable	−25
White Settler	−200

SUCCESSFUL DEFORCEMENT

AFTER ALL IS SAID and done, I think the real meaning of being "local" is in shared roots—a cultural memory of earlier life and events that shape Coigach today.

Nineteenth century Coigach is a story of people living at the margin of subsistence with famine always at the door. The land was poor, agricultural practice was primitive, and families were large. Four or five children provided a form of old age insurance. Poverty and deprivation were accepted as normal, and survival depended on mutual support when things were bad.

According to historians, what a family was able to grow on two or three acres and the sale of a beast or two each year produced about half of what they needed to subsist on. Those who could manage to do so traveled outside the district for part of each year to work for cash. "The people are all poor together as they must necessarily be; they go away to Caithness to the herring fishing, and look out for such kind of work as they can undertake."

Even so, many crofters were always in arrears on their land rent and in debt for food they bought on credit, ordinarily from the landlord. Potatoes were the basic subsistence crop, and a bad year meant near starvation. A disastrous potato blight began in 1847 and lasted until 1850. Since allowing tenants to die by starvation was considered bad form, Coigach landlords created employment schemes based on building "destitution roads." This provided relief "for the able bodied among the destitute" without calling it relief, because "unrestrained charity" was viewed as a "moral danger to both recipient and donor." And then there was the added virtue that road work would "educate people into regular habits of work and provide a taste of comforts that hitherto they had not discovered the want of." And if that wasn't enough, "The road work will teach them to work with pick and spade which is a valuable species of education for them through life."

While there were good years such as 1851 when potato yields were high, herring catches plentiful, and cash jobs to be had all round the Highlands, there were bad years in each decade when potato crops failed—1861–63, 1870, 1872, 1881, and 1885. Each subsistence crisis called for relief for Coigach crofters, and road schemes came to the rescue. The results were that no one died of starvation, a somewhat formal relief system was created, and roads connecting Coigach to the outside world were completed.

The 1850s in Coigach were notable for another reason: the resistance of tenants who successfully defied landlords and the law to retain their crofts. The crofters' small plots, and cottages they built on them stone by stone, represented what little security and margin of dignity they had. In 1852, the Marquis of Stafford ordered forty long-time tenants off the land. It was "to be put under sheep" to produce high-er returns. The tenants refused and threatened "deforcement," which my 1933 Oxford Universal Dictionary defines as "preventing by force [an officer of the law] from executing his official duty."

This was the story of the affair as told by Margaret MacLeod to her grandson and recounted by him at age eighty-four. Margaret MacLeod was sixteen when she participated in the "deforcement."

When the Sheriff's men came to Ullapool on their way to Coigach [by boat] to serve the summons, a young lad named Gordon came quickly along the coast and told the people. A large crowd gathered on the beach below the hotel at Achiltibuie where the boat landed. A number of the teenage girls and some teenage boys dressed as girls then caught hold of the Sheriff's men and stripped them, looking for the sum-mons. They failed to find them on their bodies. Then they searched the boat. They found them nailed under the sole at the stern. The summons was taken and burnt there and then in bonfire on the beach. Then one of the lassies was put sitting in the stern and the boat carried shoulder high in triumph for about a quarter of a mile and dumped on top of the potato pit just below the hotel and left there. No doubt a drink or two would be taken to celebrate the victory, for the local cellar was only about fifty yards from the potato pit.

Another storyteller has the boat burned on the beach and the Sheriff's men forced to walk back to Ullapool without their pants in what was known in local lore as "The March of the Cold Testicles."

Reflecting on his interviews with locals, Angus MacLeod notes that while most locals got around to talking about the deforcement, the tale has not assumed a central place in the life of the people. It is not ritually told on that special day of the year. There is no ceremony to mark it. This made me wonder if, among a proud people, pride isn't fullest and deepest when it is not put on public display. What is most important to present day Coigach is that locals have retained for themselves and infused incomers with a spirit of independence, mutual help, and cooperation. Coigach retains a unique character and a degree of isolation that allows it to be both a part of and apart from the modern world.

Thinking back, I wonder if it isn't the profound beauty that transcends all else. I know it did for G and me. We became captives of Coigach.

Captives of Coigach

THIS SECTION COULD HAVE also have been titled, "A Marvelous Amount of Nothing to Do."

Ten miles north of Ullapool on the A835, turning west just after Strathcanaird, we began fifteen very slow, twisting miles on single-track roads along the base of Stac Pollaidh (The Pitted Stack) in the Inverpolly Nature Reserve. We saw a few healthy-looking people setting out for challenging climbs on trails to Linneraineach (Pool of Ferns), Lochan Fhionnlaidh (Small Pale Lake), and Allt an Loin Dubh (Stream of the Dark Glade). We waved a hello and they waved back. Everyone waves to everyone in the North West Highlands.

We drove along deep blue freshwater lochs of Lurgainn, Bad a'Ghaill and Osgain that border the road and run one into the other. Not another car or person was in sight and Gaelic songs on our tape player resonated to the lochs and gorse-covered moors.

A ghillean oga eisdibh
    O young lads now listen

Gus 'n dean mi sgeula aithris dhuibh
> While I tell you my tale

Oir feumaidh mi bhith fagail
> For I must be leaving

An tir a dharaich m' athraichean
> The land where my ancestors were reared

Then south at Achna'haird Beach, where the very narrow road narrowed even more, past Loch Raa and Loch Vatachan and then, in the words of any self-respecting brochure—the vast panorama of the Summer Isles opened before our eyes with the white cottages of Achiltibuie (Ahh il tee boo wy) strung out along the shore.

We checked into the very highly rated and "sophisticated" Summer Isles Hotel, originally built in the early 1800s as a guesthouse

SUMMER ISLES HOTEL
MENU

~

Mousse of Lemon Sole
served with a fresh granary loaf

~

Carpaccio of Aberdeen Angus Beef Filet
served with piquant relish

~

Fresh Summer Isles Lobster
with mixed herbs and a light butter sauce

~

Sweet Trolley

~

Selection of Fine Cheeses

~

Coffee

for the Cromertie estate. The view from our room spread across Badentarbat Bay to Tanera Mor, one of the islands where large sheep and little lambs go in small boats to pasture through the summer. Mark and Gerry Irvine rescued the hotel from near bankruptcy in 1987 after Mark's father Robert had drained hotel resources into a vision, the Hydroponicum, a glorified subtropical greenhouse that grows exotic fruit and plants hydroponically (without soil). The greenhouse sits across the road from the hotel and, to be generous, it is a blight on the landscape, looking rather like a giant Quonset or dirigible hangar covered with dirty plastic. Other than a large hotel dominating Lochinver, it is one of the few eyesores we saw in the North West Highlands. It stands out in a world where there are no billboards, no drive-ins, just lochs, moors, mountains, and buildings that may not be architectural gems but look like they belong.

The hotel has comfortable lounges, furnishings in good taste, masses of fresh flowers, and a grass-roofed annex, and to boot, the Irvines are very thoughtful hosts. While the hotel brochure states there is little formality, it also notes, "Most guests like to change for dinner." The dining room and chef are well-known, and the five course dinners, though a bit pricey, are a worthwhile experience. For those so inclined there is an excellent wine cellar. We "changed" for dinner and enjoyed all five courses.

In one of those curious conjunctions of life, the best single dish of our trip came the next night at an unprepossessing bar, the Am Fuaran in Altandhu, a couple miles up the peninsula from the hotel. Décor included the requisite pool table, dartboard, and television above the bar tuned to a soccer match. The clientele was local. As best we could make out, the kitchen was in the house next door, since the chef/waitress entered and exited through an outside door behind the bar. She was sweet, short, and wore a flowery dress. The dish: fresh local shrimp in a Thai ginger garlic sauce. It was wonderful.

ARTIST'S SENSE AND SOUL

WHEN I TALKED WITH Gerry Irvine about the area, she told me about the fishing and hiking and trips around the Summer Isles on the Hectoria, but felt the best part of Coigach was "a marvelous amount of nothing to do." Nothing except to let it all in—the silence, the color, and the shimmering light over the water. All this combines to clear one's head wonderfully and impart a remarkable sense of safety and peace. I never once felt the need to read a newspaper.

I asked G what most touched her artist's sense and soul. This is what spoke to her:

"Seeing the morning sun burn mist off the islands, leaving little puffs of mist here and there...the golden light of a late tranquil afternoon transformed in the early evening to a fine luminescent glow...swirling graceful patterns on the surface of the loch...a lovely kind of silence with soft wind on the water."

My favorite place was a washed-up log next to the remains of a stone cottage at the western end of the peninsula. Sitting there, I would look over Reiff Bay across a wide ocean channel to the Island of Lewis and beyond. Sit there long enough with a few sea birds and a couple of lambs as company, and you have a world of your own.

On the way back from Reiff we were held up at a "lamb crossing." Two shepherds and their sheep dogs were guiding a flock of wobbly, newborn lambs and their unconcerned mothers down a hill and across the road to new pasture. After a chat about this and that, one of the shepherds asked me how I thought "your new president" was doing. "Better, I hope," I said.

G's favorite place was a view from the road that circles the top of the peninsula. The road begins just after Altandhu (Dark Burn) and runs north, slowly climbing the moor. At the highest point of the moor, before the road drops down to the Brae of Achnahaird (Field on the Point), there is a classic view—Stac Pollaidh, Col Mor, Cul Beag, and Beinn Mor Coigach, 800 million years in the making, rising one by one from an undulating landscape of moor and marsh.

Each of these mountains has a loch at its base and a personality of its own. Suilven and Canisp stand alone in the misty background. We live in Colorado at five thousand feet a couple of blocks from the foot of the Rockies, whose overwhelming peaks rise to fourteen thousand feet. These three Highland mountains, the highest at 2,750 feet, are very different. You feel you can get to know them.

From Coigach we were off on the "wee mad road" to Lochinver.

The Perfect Walk and Other Wonders
Suilven, Scallops, Serendipity, Grateful Toads, and the Lighthouse Stevensons

ATLANTIC OCEAN

Handa Island

Scourie

EDDRACHILLIS
BAY

Point of Stoer

Stoer Head Lighthouse

Quinag 2654 ft.

Clachtoll

Clachtoll - a lovely little, colorful beach

The Albannach Suilven in our room

Lochan Ordain - of Toads and Princes

River Inver

Loch Assynt

Baddidarroch

The perfect Walk

Lochinver

Beinn Gharbh 1769 ft.

Hand-Dived Scallops

Inverkirkaig

Suilven 2399 ft.

Canisp 2779 ft.

Serendipity and Song

The "Wee Mad Road" it does so concentrate the mind

Cul Mor 2787 ft.

N

Loch
Two lane road
Single track road

0   2   4
miles

AR

CHAPTER FIVE

LOCHINVER, SUILVEN, TOADS, AND A LIGHTHOUSE

IT DOES SO CONCENTRATE THE MIND

WE ARE OFF TO Lochinver and Baddidarroch (Baddy **dar** ro hh) and an intimate view of Suilven.

We headed north past Cul Beag and Cul Mor on what the locals refer to affectionately as the "wee mad road." *The Rough Guide* describes this single track adventure as "unremittingly spectacular, threading its way through a tumultuous landscape of secret valleys, moorland, and bare rock." G says that description is a little high on the hyperbole but not far off the mark. I have to take her word for it because my eyes were fixed most carefully on the road. I was hugging the right edge around the curving base of a steep hill because a few feet over from the left side of the car there was an abrupt drop into the deep waters of Lochan Eisg-brachaidh. This sort of situation does so concentrate the mind. I found another disarming characteristic of the wee mad road was steep grades here and there that directed the car bonnet (hood) toward heaven, leaving me without a prayer of seeing ahead.

I was told there are very few accidents on this or other single-track roads. The reasons may be that these roads cry out for careful driving, and a near-universal adherence to single-track driving protocols based on "blips." To get the picture, visualize a number of spots where the road bumps out, creating a blip large enough for one car to pull off and let another car pass. Single-track rules work in large part because cars move at relatively slow speeds.

Rule #1: When two cars are on course for a head-on collision, the first driver to reach a blip on his (please read his/her) side of the road pulls off, stops, and lets the other car go by. If there is no blip on your side of the road and you get to where there is one is on the other side, pull up and wait for the oncoming driver to swing into his blip and around your car. You do not ever pull into a blip on the other side of the road unless you are using the blip to take an unforgettable picture. Scots will know you are a visitor and they tend to be forgiving.

Rule #2: If cars meet on a blind curve, the driver on the inside backs up to the nearest blip. Fortunately, this never happened to me. I found backing up a car with a right hand drive ran counter to all my instincts.

Rule #3: If you have any sense, you drive more slowly than a local driver who is familiar with the road. If a local driver comes up behind you (and they never honk), pull off at the first blip on your side and let him pass.

Rule #4: The Wave. This is absolutely essential and is the essence of good single-track manners. Your hands are fixed firmly on the steering wheel in a race driver's grip, left hand at 10:00 and right hand at 2:00. You come up to a car waiting in a blip for you to pass or you are in a blip to let another car go by, cars pull abreast of each other, drivers' eyes meet, both raise four fingers of their right hand (thumb does not leave steering wheel) in a mutual salute. Thank you. You're welcome. The Wave is accompanied by a nod and a smile as strangers pass in the day. I never drove at night.

Ewes, lambs, and Highland cattle have no regard for single-track protocols, so you just have to wait them out.

SUILVEN IN OUR ROOM

IT IS A BIT of a shock to emerge from the raw and isolated universe of the wee mad road, swing around sheltered Badnaban Bay into the working village of Lochinver, and see factory-like Lochinver Harbor dominating the entire south shore of the village. The harbor is an international whitefish and langoustines port linked to Northeast Atlantic fishing. Boats of every size from one-man inshore shellfish creel boats to huge, deep-sea trawlers are docked at piers with towering cranes unloading tons of fish from these big boats. Three big, metal-clad warehouse buildings dominate the scene—a grading and packing center, an eight thousand square foot auction hall with Internet connections to buyers all over Europe, and a tower grinding out eighty thousand tons of ice a day. Refrigerator trucks from France, Spain, Norway, and big cities in the U.K., coolers humming, are lined up ready to be loaded while men off the fishing boats do much the same in the two waterfront bars.

The port was financed with European Union funds. The curiosity, I was told, is that with this major fishing port opening in the 1990s, the pattern is fresh fish out, frozen fish in. It has become increasingly difficult to buy fresh fish locally, unless you have good connections, as was the case of the guesthouse where we stayed.

With a population of 558, Lochinver is a large village by North West Highlands standards. We continued along the bay—one hotel, two restaurants, three bars, several bed-and-breakfasts, a grocery, an unfortunately placed waterfront petrol station, a small park—then over a graceful stone bridge where the River Inver rushes into Loch Inver. Then a sharp left, and on a half mile to the coastal township of Baddidarroch and the Albannach, a four-star establishment variously defined by *Guide Michelin* and *Scotland the Best!* as a "five room hotel with an excellent restaurant" or an "excellent restaurant with rooms." And there it was, just as described, "A nineteenth-century house of great character, standing proudly on a gentle hill in a south-facing garden with spectacular views across the bay of the Assynt Mountains and Suilven's extraordinary dome looming large."

Lesley Crosfield and her longtime partner, Colin Craig, found the crumbling Albannach a dozen years ago and scrubbed, sawed, hammered, painted, furnished, and cooked it into existence and award-winning recognition. Lesley, who always seemed to answer the phone while cooking (it turned out she spent at least eight hours day in the kitchen), had promised me a room that Suilven came right into—and it did, most impressively.

The mountain Suilven was our constant companion. From our room, the conservatory, or the terrace, or as we drove around, there was Suilven emerging from the morning mist, changing by the moment in the day's light. Suilven is the only mountain I ever met that generates affection, and it comes from travelers and writers as well as locals. G, with her artist's sight and soul, was first attracted to Suilven many years ago when she was looking at pictures of Scotland, and here it was.

Viewed from our room, the north face of Suilven looked like a British policeman's helmet. When we saw Suilven from the east, it looked spiky, a bit like something out of a Hollywood moonscape. From the southwest the top looked like a bumpy ridge with high points at both ends and a droop in the middle. The west peak, Caisteal Liath, rises to 2,398 feet, and the east peak, Meall Meadhonach (Hill of the Maiden) to 2,372 feet. The droop in the middle of the two, Bealach Mor, is at 1,673 feet a drop of more than seven hundred feet from either end. One climber we spoke with said Bealach Mor was a bit of a surprise and felt like "a gently sloping grass field perched on the top of the world."

The name Suilven comes from the Norse and means "Pillar Mountain," a perspective Vikings would have had from the sea. The mountain has been nearly a billion years in the making. Small by mountain standards, the mass of reddish- brown Torridonian sandstone rises abruptly from a rolling base of Lewisian gneiss with lochans (small lakes) all round. Seen from the Albannach in the morning sun, the dusting of gray quartzite at the top looked like a cover of snow, and in the evening light like a silver dome.

HAND-DIVED SCALLOPS

THERE IS ONE ADVANTAGE of corresponding via fax and e-mail and speaking with innkeepers by phone in the process of making a reservation and clarifying Creaky needs. When you arrive you have the feeling of visiting a friend. Three days with Lesley and Colin only reinforced this feeling.

Over tea in the conservatory and sherry on the terrace, we got a bit of history. After art school and the end of an early marriage, Lesley was running a hotel in the Trossachs, a mountain area near Loch Lomond, and dreaming of meals she wanted to cook. Enter Colin, tall, bearded, muscular, looking like he just came from caber tossing (heaving a seventeen-foot log as far as you can) in the Highland games. He was then manager of an electronics factory in the dot-com area the Scots call Silicon Glen and not all that happy with the job. Lesley discovered that Colin was also a devoted cook with a taste for the odd dram and a deep knowledge of good wines. Their partnership blossomed at a Hogmanay (New Year's Eve celebration dating back to pagan rituals worshipping fire and sun), which Lesley put on with music, singing, and appropriate beverages that achieved the flavor of Louis MacNeice's poem "Bagpipe Music."

> The Laird of Phelps spent Hogmanay
> Declaring he was sober
> Counted his feet to prove the fact
> And found he had one foot over

In 1989, two years after the Hogmanay party, Lesley and Colin found the Albannach, and today there isn't a polished brass fixture or a carefully chosen piece of furniture that doesn't bear their mark. In my trip journal I came across a note about Lesley saying locals accepted them because "we put on our boiler suits and mucked in." I e-mailed, "Please clarify." Colin did.

"The boiler suit mystery is easily resolved. It's merely a one-piece coverall, a working garment traditionally worn by engineers. In our case it is the mucking in uniform of our do-it-ourselves build/renovate/decorate/landscape winter work program, dispelling notions of 'privileged' incomers as we are usually dirtier than any builder." (Muckers work in mines with pick and shovel, clearing away underground debris.)

Colin and Lesley share cooking duties, and Colin presents the food in full kilt. Dinner is by candlelight in a wood-paneled dining room. From our window table we could see Suilven across the bay fading slowly into the good night, which in the North West Highlands in May is around 10:00 or so. The setting and the kitchen do each other proud. Here is one of the glorious dinners we had at the Albannach.

Incidentally, hand-dived scallops are what Colin fetches when he puts on his wet suit and flippers and dives into Badnaban Bay from a creel boat run by a friend.

ALBANNACH MENU

~

Seared, hand-dived Badnaban Scallops and
Pan-Fried Duck Livers, with Mixed Leaves

~

Red Pepper Soufflé with Red Onion Marmalade

~

Baked Fillet of Lochinver-Landed Halibut on Leeks
and Sorrel, with Vegetables in Salsa Verde, Asparagus,
Fennel Potatoes and Hollandaise Sauce

~

Cashel Blue and Ardracharn Cheeses

~

Lemon and Lime Torte with Orange Caramel
and Berry Fruit Basket

~

Coffee

THE PERFECT WALK

All things by immortal power,
Near or far,
Hiddenly
To each other linked are,
That thou canst not stir a flower
Without troubling of a star

—FRANCIS THOMPSON

THE WATER OF LOCH Assynt runs toward the sea, dropping first into two small lochans, then to the River Inver, and finally to Loch Inver. For the last half-mile or so before the river rushes under the stone highway bridge into the loch, a narrow dirt path runs along the south bank, and on the other side of the river the rocky north bank rises steeply. Large and small rocks have broken off, fallen, and rolled into the river, fashioning quiet ponds, furious whirlpools, narrow passages, and small falls—the water's movement creating a wonderful variety of sounds and patterns. The riverbanks and hillside were filled with masses of ferns, mosses, orchids, heather, and bilberry.

Light green spring leaves of birch and willow trees filtered and reflected the sun onto lichen-covered rocks bordering the path. We ambled, stopped, stared, and laughed a lot. We had it all to ourselves. It was the perfect walk.

This was one of those rare occasions when small things come together to create feelings of pleasure, peace, and happiness that are long remembered, especially when the moment is shared with a person you love deeply. Then, all's right with the world.

Serendipity Was Our Companion

WITH OUR WALK OVER, it was time for tea, and we decided to head for Achins Book Shop and Coffee Shop at Inverkirkaig, just south of Lochinver at the end (or beginning) of the wee mad road. The shop sits on a hill between Suilven and the sea where the path to Kirkaig Falls begins.

When we entered the shop the now familiar Gaelic lament "Turning Your Back on Assynt" ("Cur culaibh ri Assainte") was playing, but what struck us was that the singer of this version had a far more haunting voice, a more soulful quality than any of the three versions of that song on tapes we had been playing.

> *From the time we left Lochinver*
> *I was in totally strange country*
> *By the time we reached Lairg*
> *Neither hill nor glen did I know*
>
> *Tonight I am so sad*
> *Walking the streets of Canada*
> *And with a cold wide ocean*
> *Between me and my love in Assynt*

We ordered tea from the proprietor Alex Dickson, and G began talking with him about Gaelic music and the tape then playing. I took my tea to a corner table and began talking about the upcoming election with two women. One's name was Agnes and I never got the name of the other, although I do remember her strongly held views. Like most Scots, she was not at all reticent about sharing them.

"Westminster does bloody nothing for us. Edinburgh may be closer, but the Scottish Parliament is useless. We need devolution. We need to run ourselves." I asked how she felt about Scotland getting funds back from Westminster in programs and grants that total about a third more than the taxes Scotland sends south. "No matter," she said. "We are a damn sight smarter and can do more with less, and what about tons of money from North Sea oil that should be ours?"

On "smarter" she may have been right. According to Havelock Ellis's *Study of British Genius,* with only ten percent of the British population Scotland has produced 15.4 percent of Britain's geniuses and twenty percent of Britain's "most eminent scientists and engineers." As to oil revenues, if, according to international law, a line is drawn out to sea that follows the border between Scotland and England, most of the oil falls on the English side of the line.

And then we got on to the subject of the Vesteys, the family that owns the land under Lochinver and a hundred thousand acres all round, including four forests (Inchnadamph, Drumrunie, Glencanisp, and Ben More), four mountains (Suilven, Canisp, Cul Mor, and Ben More), three salmon rivers (Kirkaig, Inver, and Oykel), Loch Assynt, and any number of other lochs and lochans. Vestey also owns the store and petrol station in town. My tea companion's comments on this: "There is Vestey with all his damn land and his ugly house and his ugly hotel high on his hill surveying all he owns and lording it over us. Don't build here. Don't build there. He takes our [land] rent money, tells us what to do, and pays no taxes. It's not fair and devolution will do away with it."

Edmund Vestey does have a controversial inheritance tax waiver exempting his four sons from death duties on land they will eventually inherit in exchange for an agreement on environmental preservation on his estate and relatively free public access. There is now a disagreement between Vestey and environmentalists as to whether the number of red deer he maintains for stalking exceeds levels of sustainability. Another sore point with the locals is Vestey's refusal to sell Lochinver one site wanted for public housing and another for a public swimming pool that would use waste heat from the port's ice plant. "Maybe now that Peter Hay, that [expletive deleted] loud-mouthed factor [estate manager] who treated us like dirty natives [Hay had been a game warden in Kenya] is being retired and one of the Vestey sons is taking over, things will get better."

About then G joined us and started talking about the wonderful tape of Agnes Dickson songs she had just bought. Alex came over

and said the singer was his wife. The outspoken woman began point-
ing to Agnes, whose confident beauty and quiet smile G and I still
remember. She was, of course, Agnes Dickson, singer and mother,
and, with Alex, proprietor of Achins. She had recorded the tape in
1994. Family took precedence, and Agnes never went on tour or
made another tape.

After that, it was back to the Albannach for a quiet read in the garden, with an occasional glance at Suilven, a game of chess, and a
before-dinner drink on the terrace.

OF TOADS AND PRINCES

THE NEXT DAY WAS overcast with a soft mist and an occasional drizzle, just right for a visit to the lighthouse at Stoer Head. After the usual
giant breakfast and a recovery period, we were off. According to my
map our destination would take us one mile on A837, a two-lane
Highland super highway, seven miles on B869, a "narrow road with
passing places," and another three miles on "other road, drive, or track."

Two miles up the B869 the road rose sharply—nearly four hundred feet—and at the crest of the hill there was a perfectly placed
viewpoint. To the southwest we had another angle on Suilven and its
near neighbor, Canisp. In any other country Canisp would get star
billing, but here Suilven is clearly top banana. Further on, Cul Mor
and our old friends of Coigach days, Cul Beag and Stac Polliadh,
completed the panoramic scene. To the north there was a very different picture, a canvas of about ten square miles filled with freshwater
lochs. Most, we were told, teamed with much-prized brown trout.
That evening I counted the lochs and lochans in the ten-square-mile
area on my ordnance survey map. The number came to 6.7 per square
mile, about seventy in all.

Downhill and a tad beyond the viewpoint was Lochan Ordain, its
surface covered with white water lilies. There at the road was a sign:

"WARNING—TOAD CROSSING." We stopped to admire the water lilies and contemplate the warning sign, wondering if the toad had already been kissed, but there was neither prince nor toad in sight. Well, in Gairloch we saw a "WARNING – ELDERLY CROSSING" sign and never saw a single elderly and now here was a toad crossing and no toads. Was this a Highland kind of thing?

THE LIGHTHOUSE STEVENSONS

Oh! dream of joy! is this indeed
The lighthouse top I see?
Is this the hill? Is this the kirk
Is this mine own countree?
                    —SAMUEL TAYLOR COLERIDGE

WE CONTINUED ALONG THE coast, stopping for a barefoot walk on the white sand beach of Clachtolla (Klahh tow la). Then it was on through the crofting townships of Totag, Balchladich, and Raffin, and on to a stretch of track, around a blind curve. There without warning was Stoer Head Lighthouse, gleaming white, solemn and proud, perched on a rocky promontory with its beacon tower aimed protectively out to the gray sea pounding relentlessly against the rugged coast below. The scene had the impact of a powerful painting in a vast, outdoor museum. It took a bit to connect this scene with its work-a-day lifesaving purpose and a history tracking back to the eighteenth century.

By the late 1700s merchant and military ships by the hundreds had perished on the rocks of northern Scotland's treacherous coast. The carnage produced an industry of "wreckers," gangs that in bad weather would listen for the sound of a ship foundering on the rocks and plunder the wrecks with no thought of helping survivors. Worse yet they caused wrecks by tying a lantern to a horse's tail and leading the horse along the shore to make it look like the swinging of a ship's light dead ahead. Finally, in 1786, the British Parliament established the Northern Lighthouse Board with funds to build four lighthouses. Thus began the fascinating legacy of the "Lighthouse Stevensons," beginning with Robert Stevenson as engineer to the Lighthouse Board.

By 1806, Stevenson had built nine lighthouses with beacon lights evolving from coal fires to multiple candles to oil lamps. Electricity came late in the century.

Robert Stevenson's three sons, David, Alan, and Tom followed in the family tradition, as did three generations beyond them, all engineers to the Northern Lighthouse Board. Brothers David and Tom were engineers for the Stoer Head Lighthouse. It was completed in 1870 and automated in 1976 after 106 years of continuous residence by successive generations of lighthouse keepers and their families. David and Thomas were uncles of Robert Louis Stevenson, who started as an engineer, tried law, and then, to the good fortune of readers everywhere, settled on a writer's career. Readers may remember that hero David Balfour in *Kidnapped* is shipwrecked on the tiny island of Erraid in the Hebrides. Erraid was where young Stevenson spent many adventurous weeks when his father and uncle David were building a lighthouse on the island.

Between 1790 and 1940, eight members of the Stevenson family planned, designed, and constructed ninety-seven manned lighthouses that still proudly dot the Scottish coast. The Lighthouse Stevensons were also responsible for many of the optic developments that made "life beams to the sea" more and more powerful. It was with good reason that Robert Louis Stevenson wrote, "Whenever I smell saltwater I know I am not far from one of the works of my ancestors."

According to Bella Bathurst, author of *The Lighthouse Stevensons*, Robert carried with him a sense of guilt over leaving Scotland and not following in the family tradition. Robert Louis Stevenson wrote this revealing poem.

> *Say not of me that weakly I declined*
> *The labours of my sires, and fled the sea,*

The towers we built and the lamps we lit,
To play at home with paper like a child
But rather say: In the afternoon of time
A strenuous family dusted from its hands
The sand of granite, and beholding far
Along the sounding coast its pyramids
And tall memorials catch the dying sun,
Smiled well content, and to this childish task
Around the fire addressed its evening hours.

G and I sat for an hour or so at a picnic table at cliff's edge just down the slope from Stoer Head Lighthouse, admiring David and Tom's work, wondering about the life of a lighthouse keeper and if, as a breed, they were avid readers. A few sheep and lambs completed the scene. There was one interruption. A car drove up, and a man and woman got out. Both took a few pictures—posing each other with the lighthouse in the background—got back in their car, and drove off. Elapsed time, three minutes. I wonder what they saw.

TOAD MYSTERY SOLVED

Assynt News
May 4, 2001

CHILDREN OF ASSYNT HELP 2,658 TOADS ACROSS ROAD

The toads, newts and frogs awoke early on 5th March and crossed B869 to Lochan Ordain to spawn until severe weather stopped amphibian activity March 20th—28th. On March 21 the Warning Toad Crossing sign was stolen. This did not result in many casualties because of the lull in toad activity.
The Assynt Field Club and our Friendly County Council came

The Assynt Field Club and our Friendly County Council came to our aid and a replacement sign was put in place. The amphibians resumed their migration, both across to the Lochan and back. The total number of toads saved by the children of Assynt staggering. Many, many amphibians owe their lives and continuance of their species to these children. They were just as keen and happy in the pouring rain with wet wellies [boots] and coats as on milder nights.

FINAL NUMBERS FOR SPRING 2001, MARCH 5th TO APRIL 27th

	Males	Females	Total
Toads Over to Lochan Ordain	1640	243	1883
Toads Returning from Locan Ordain	651	124	775
Total Toads Helped Across the Road	2291	367	2658
Number Killed Over and Back	146	26	192

The story in the *Assynt News* also reported that of the twenty-nine Assynt (**Ass** ent) children ages five to sixteen in the Toad Patrol, eight (27.6 percent) were MacLeods. This is only appropriate, since the Lochinver area of Assynt is the ancestral home of the Clan MacLeod.

As I reread the news story and studied the statistics, a number of questions came to mind. Several transatlantic telephone conversations with Erica Gorman, leader of the expedition, revealed this essential information. (1) Early evening toad migration always begins "after the last thrush sings," but never when there is a full moon, because then the owls would eat them. Males cross first, their melodious trills wooing females to follow. (2) Toads come to Loch Ordain from a mile or more around because of the water lilies covering the lake. Toads string their spawn around lily pad roots, ensuring them a high survival rate even in the worst winters. (3) Toads are easy to sex because females are bigger than males. (4) The count going over is likely to be more accurate than the return count for several reasons. Toads move more slowly and hop less going over because they have just come out of hibernation and are still sleepy. Also, some toads cross back late at night when younger counters in the Toad Patrol are home asleep.

I was not able to get an answer to one perplexing question. If the reason for going to Lochan Ordain (Lohha **Nord** an) is to spawn, why is the ratio of male to female toads six to one? Protection? Polygamy? Nature's fertilization guarantee?

The Gormans are also incomers to the Highlands. Erica told me that after years of "yearning to live in Sutherland," in 1996 she and John discovered The Old Poor House in the crofting township of Torbreck near Lochinver. The house had been built in 1847 as an "accommodation of paupers." Considering what it took to fix it up, the Gormans felt the pauper designation was certainly appropriate. After moving in they discovered their garden and surrounding land was a breeding ground for toads and were shocked by the mortality rate of toads crossing the B869 at spawning time.

Moving into action the Gormans registered the site first with the Herpetofauna Society and then with the Ministry of Transport to erect a toad crossing sign. Next came a grant from Care for the Wild International to pay for ministry-approved toad crossing signs. The Toad Patrol, which included nearly half of all fifty-six Lochinver Primary School students, was next, and it has been a great success for both toads and kids. Many more toads get to live. For the kids, in addition to the satisfaction of saving toad lives and becoming junior statisticians, they get to stay up late, direct traffic and get close to nighttime wildlife—hooting owls, the soft shrill whistle of otters, bats hawking for insects, and the drumming of common snipes.

A NEW CREAKY TRAVELER AWARD

AFTER WE HAD ANOTHER superior breakfast and an interval on the terrace communing with Suilven, Lesley and Colin helped us out with suitcases to our car, in a special parking spot next to the Albannach they had cleared so G and I wouldn't have to walk up a small hill from the regular parking lot. Lesley and Colin wished us well, and as they waved us off it occurred to me that a new type of award was in order. Four stars and the Bib Gourmand from *Guide Michelin* are fine and dandy, but there is a dimension in the quality of a stay not ordinarily addressed. To correct this serious omission, I now award to Lesley Crosfield and Colin Craig of the Albannach, to Di Johnson and Inge Ford of Little Lodge, and to Lesley Black of Port-Na-Con Guest House:

THE CREAKY TRAVELER AWARD
For thoughtful, kind, warm, and
considerate innkeeper performance.

And so we were off to Scourie, where an island for the birds, a tired palm tree, and ten beady-eyed langoustines awaited us. On the way were new insights into more than a thousand years of Highland history.

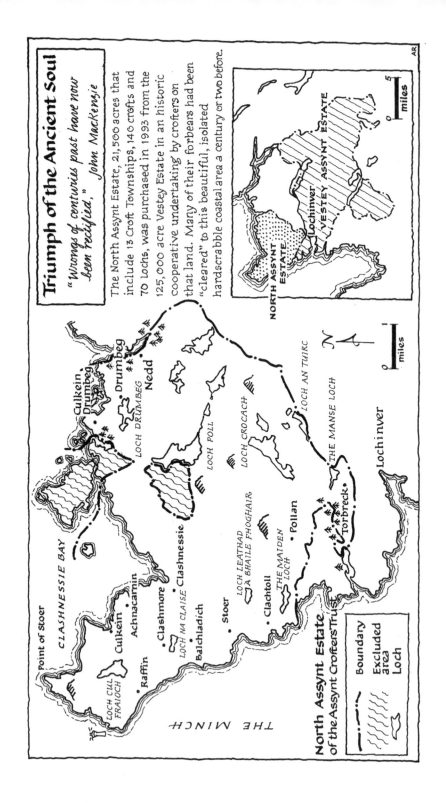

Triumph of the Ancient Soul

"Wrongs of centuries past have now been rectified," John MacKenzie

The North Assynt Estate, 21,500 acres that include 13 Croft Townships, 140 crofts and 70 Lochs, was purchased in 1993 from the 125,000 acre Vestey Estate in an historic cooperative undertaking by crofters on that land. Many of their forbears had been "cleared" to this beautiful, isolated hardscrabble coastal area a century or two before.

NORTH ASSYNT ESTATE

VESTEY ASSYNT ESTATE

Lochinver

0 5 miles

THE MINCH

CLASHNESSIE BAY

Point of Stoer

Culkein Drumbeg

Drumbeg

Nedd

LOCH DRUMBEG

LOCH POLL

LOCH CROCACH

LOCH AN TUIRC

THE MANSE LOCH

Lochinver

Culkein

Achnacarnin

Clashmore

LOCH NA CLAISE Clashnessie

Balchladich

Raffin

LOCH CULL FRAIOCH

Stoer

LOCH LEATHAD A BHAILE FHOGHAIR

Clachtoll

THE MAIDEN LOCH

Pollan

Torbreck

N

0 1 miles

North Assynt Estate
of the Assynt Crofters Trust

Boundary

Excluded area

Loch

AR

CHAPTER SIX

BEYOND THE CLEARANCES

WE HAVE WON THE LAND

DRIVING TO SCOURIE, WE naturally chose the narrow single track that hugs the fjord-like coast. This road is referred to by locals as the Breakdown Zone, because its "ups and downs claim so many victims." In comparison, the wee mad road from Coigach to Lochinver was a piece of cake.

Our leisurely drive took us past Lochan Ordain, all covered with white water lilies, and then to a soft white sand beach set against the turquoise water of the tiny Bay of Clachtoll where we had spent a wonderfully drowsy afternoon. A few miles further on a signpost to Achnacarnin triggered thoughts of the eighteenth- and nineteenth-century Assynt clearances. Families were "cleared" by landlords from fertile glens (valleys) and forced to start again, some in America, others on small mean crofts along the rocky Highland coast.

> Over fifty townships in this parish were made desolate, and the
> tenants sent hither and thither over the face of the earth, and
> when they found a resting place at all in their native land, it was

on the poorest scraps, rocks, and bogs and often put in amongst the poorest crofters, subdividing their lots, and intensifying their poverty.

—WILLIAM MACKENZIE OF CLASHNESSIE
Testimony to the Napier
Commission, 1883

This list of fourteen families "cleared" from fertile lands of Unapool to the rocky coast of Achnacarnin and to America gave me a human measure of William Mackenzie's testimony. The clan names—eight Mackenzie, four Macdonald, two Macrae—speak volumes of the callous abuse of clan loyalty that had been generations in the making.

Destination of Households Cleared from Unapool in 1820*

Household	Males	Females	Destination
Donald Mackenzie(a)	4	1	Achnacarnin
Donald MacRae	1	1	Achnacarnin
Donald Macdonald	5	2	Achnacarnin
Donald Mackenzie(b)	2	4	Achnacarnin
D. Mackenzie's widow	1	2	Achnacarnin
John MacLeod	2	5	Achnacarnin
Alexander MacRae	1	2	Achnacarnin
Neil Mackenzie	3	1	America
Alexander Mackenzie	4	4	America
Donald Macdonald	1	2	America
John Mackenzie	2	3	America
Simon Mackenzie	3	1	America
Murdoch Macdonald	4	3	America
Alexander Mackenzie	3	2	America
	37	33	

*Malcolm Bangor-Jones, *The Assynt Clearances*

Inverness—Across the River Inver from Ness Bank

Little Lodge on Gair Loch, North Erradale

Loch Maree as Queen Victoria saw it

The far side of Loch Maree—Slioch and Sgurr Dubn

Loch Ewe—lambs, new and very new

In memory of Our Shipmates, World War II convoys

Clan Chief—two feet tall and ready for battle

Coigach: Single track to contemplation

Evening over the Summer Isles

Coigach: Beach at Achnahaird Bay

"Water painting" on Badentarbat Bay

Coigach View: Stac Pollaidh, Cul Mor and Cul Beag

A wee bit of the wee mad road

Suilven, across Loch Inver from the garden of the Albannach

Beach at the bay of Clachtoll

G on the perfect walk

Five miles on from the turning to Achnacarnin, near the head of Loch Nedd, we stopped for a wonderful long view south, down the green fertile Abhainn Gleainn Leireag river valley. A small roadside sign, with white lettering on a bright blue background, caught my attention. Its message brought the painful drama of the Assynt clearances near full circle to a better ending.

A – ASSYNT
C – CROFTERS'
T — TRUST

The North Assynt Estate extending to 21,500 acres was purchased by inhabitants from a foreign landowner in February 1993, the first transaction of its kind in the history of crofting in the Scottish Highlands. The purchase price of £300,000 gave the people on the land control of a small part of the territory lost after the collapse of the clan system and the subsequent policy of land clearance practiced by the Duke of Sutherland. The crofters now own the land together with the mineral, fishing and shooting rights. The purchase price was raised by local and worldwide donation with grant and loan assistance from the Regional Council and public agencies. You can help by donation and purchasing fishing permits from post offices, the tourist information center and the Trust's office in Stoer.

The "foreign landowner" referred to in the ACT sign is the Englishman Edmund Vestey. The North Assynt Estate was originally a part of the 120,000-plus acres the Vestey family assembled beginning in the 1930s, largely through purchases from W. Filmer-Sankey, who had been given the estate by the Duke of Westminster as a wedding present. Years before these lochs, mountains, forests, and glens had been part of the First Duke of Sutherland's holdings of one-and-a-third million Highland acres, at a time when only 118 people owned fifty percent of Scotland. Queen Victoria summed up this pattern of ownership in her book *More Leaves,* in which she wrote of a meeting with Sir Kenneth Mackenzie of Gairloch, "He has an immense property about here, and all round is the Mackenzie country."

In 1989 Vestey split off the 21,500 acres from his larger holding, called it North Lochinver Estate, and put the property on the block in three lots. Advertising stressed unspoiled scenery, boating, "a paradise for those who love wilderness and abundant wildlife"—all the essentials of a sporting estate. With a minimum sale price of £750,000 ($1.1 million) and annual income from land rents at £2,608 ($3,910), the estate could hardly be promoted as a business proposition, especially at a time when "trophy estates" in the Highlands were just the thing for rock stars, oil-rich Arabs, and other multimillionaires. Unfortunately, as John MacAskill pointed out in his story of the purchase, *We Have Won the Land,* Vestey treated the human dimension of the North Lochinver Estate sale as incidental. Little interest was expressed in the needs and potential of the people who gave life to this area of the Assynt Estate.

The border of the estate runs from the Point of Stoer eastward along the coast to Loch Nedd, then southwest toward Lochinver and back up the coast to Stoer Head. The 21,500 acres include Achnacarnin and twelve other crofting townships with a total population of four hundred. Of these men, women, and children, three hundred live in 140 croft households (150 households were cleared to this coastal strip nearly two hundred years before), and a hundred people in other homes. The buyer of the estate, Scandinavian Property Services, a Swedish company, became their landlord, but not for long. SPS went belly-up, the estate returned to Vestey, and

Vestey put it back on the market in 1992, this time in seven parcels. The prospect of fragmentation, going from one landlord to seven, shook and energized the croft community. After seven months of intense negotiation and fundraising, crofters of the North Lochinver Estate who made up the newly created Assynt Crofters' Trust were able to pop champagne corks and proclaim, "We have won the land."

The day after the deal was done, Bill Richie, one of the prime movers, talked about his feelings. "The next day, walking out over the land, it was just awesome. To think we had actually pulled it off, that this was the first time ever . . . crofters could get up in the morning and say 'this is ours.' That was a huge, magnificent feeling."

Another key figure in the Trust, John MacKenzie, reminisced about his forbears, who had been cleared in 1819 from Inchnadamph to Culkein Drumbeg, where John now lives. John was able to point out stones that remained from the hard labor of his ancestors to bring their marginal land into production, "but they had no rights." These stones, he said, were a stark and poignant reminder of the clearances and conditions crofters endured to scratch even part of their subsistence from the land. Speaking for all crofters, Richie saw trust ownership of the land and fishing, hunting, and mineral rights of the North Lochinver Estate as a realization of a "dream that wrongs of centuries past could now be rectified."

The strong link of a crofter to "his" land has deep roots in the Celtic heritage of the Highlands with its unity of community, earth, and spirit. Trying to summarize over a thousand years in a few paragraphs is something like a performance by the Reduced Shakespeare Company of *The Complete Works of William Shakespeare (Abridged)* in 110 minutes, but here goes—tribe to clan to landlord and crofter as tennant, and in the case of the North Lochinver Estate, back to the crofter as owner. (See Appendix II for more detail.)

LIFE, LAND, AND LAW: 864 TO 2002 (ABRIDGED)

THE 140 WORKING CROFTS, thirteen crofting townships of the North Lochinver Estate, and nearly two thousand other working crofts share a way of life woven from several historic threads—centuries of tribal and clan land use, landlord-driven clearances and forced resettlement on marginal lands, crofter revolts, nineteenth- and twentieth-century laws intended to redress the balance between crofters and their landlords, and now, in recent years, a broad range of government grants and schemes to sustain and enhance crofting as a way of life.

Celts came from Ireland in the fifth century and established a small Scot kingdom. In 864, after four hundred years of war with the Picts, Kenneth MacAlpine became king of the Scots and Picts. With this, the domination of Gaelic language and culture over the whole of Scotland took root in a tribal society that held all land in common. Beginning in 1057, with Malcolm Canmore on the throne, common tribal ownership of land was replaced by a feudal system of lord and vassal, with legal ownership of large blocks of land granted by the king to individuals of his choosing, mostly from England and the Lowlands.

After the eighteen-year Scottish-English wars of independence, from 1296 to 1314, land was reallocated to Scottish patriots who fought against the English. Thus began clan society, another form of society that involved common possession of land, in which clansmen fought for their chief and in return received his protection and the guarantee of land to work. By the seventeenth century, after warring among themselves, clan chiefs had established territories and proceeded to give permanent leases of land to sons and relatives. They in turn sublet land to clan members as "tenants at will." Tenants could be moved about, but it was an article of faith that clansmen and their families would always have enough land for crops and livestock for subsistence living. According to Mara Freeman, the attachment to land, beginning with the Celts, had a deep spiritual quality involving "close cooperation with the Divine and forces of nature essential to survival . . . and a love of family and community."

In the early eighteenth century the bonds of clanship eroded. Highland clan chiefs became landlords (lairds). The economic, social, and intellectual ferment of the Scottish Enlightenment encouraged, and to a degree justified, steps lairds took to consolidate small subsistence farming plots into larger commercial sheep farms. At the same time better roads and better communication introduced Highland lairds to the high life of the Lowlands. Because of their need for more money to maintain social status—keeping up with the MacJoneses— the lairds accelerated the clearance of tenants from fertile lands the former clansmen had worked for generations.

Many families emigrated overseas. Others went to "crofts," plots of rocky land for garden crops and grazing a few cattle; these crofts were too small and harsh for living even at a subsistence level. To survive, crofters also had to work at jobs for cash, such as fishing or collecting seaweed for fertilizer, more often than not for the laird who had cleared them. Crofters had no security of tenure, even if they improved their rented croft and built a home on it. Fertile lands from which crofters had been cleared were turned into sheep farms and, when these failed, into hunting estates.

The cruelty of the clearances and the plight of croft families, including periods of famine, led to a succession of legislation beginning with the Crofters Holdings Act of 1888. This legislation provided security of tenure, fair croft rents, and the right to pass crofts on to children or relatives. More recently there has been a shift from fairness and equity for crofters to emphasis on the survival of crofting and crofting townships as a way of life in the North West Highlands.

Full Circle

After all is said and done, as T. M. Devine wrote in The Scottish Nation, "The old structure of land ownership has survived with few alterations . . .. A core of fewer than 1,500 private estates have owned most of Scotland during the last nine centuries." William Gladstone's strategy in the Crofters Holdings Act of 1888 was to make major concessions to crofters and their supporters while maintaining those basic rights of private property that were essential to the "maintenance of the social hierarchy" and their right to rule. In Parliament Gladstone argued that crofters had an historic right to the land reaching back to tribal and clan custom of common ownership, but it had been "expropriated by commercial proprietors." The crofters, Gladstone said, had been "surreptitiously deprived" of their rights to the land "to the injury of the community." So Gladstone's law gave the crofters new rights, but not the land. And all the reforms that followed in the nineteenth and twentieth centuries offered many improvements for crofters, but not the land. With their purchase of the North Lochinver Estate, the Assynt crofters did finally "get the land."

As a historian (abridged), I see three strands coming together in the deep feelings and great energy that fueled the effort of Assynt crofters. The first strand is the cultural memory of tribal and clan rights to "their" land. It is what V. S. Naipaul has called "the ancient soul." Second, within the living memory of older crofters, was the struggle of their forbears for enough land, however poor, on which to survive. Third—and this is possibly the strongest strand—has been the pursuit of dignity denied and a deep desire for control of destiny that can come only when the land has been returned to communal ownership so it is "ours," not the landlord's.

Since 1993 the Assynt Crofters' Trust has launched a sophisticated hydroelectric operation, developed several forestry projects, improved access to fishing, attracted more tourists (including American Elderhostel groups), and initiated a high-tech environmental management scheme. Beyond pride, tangible results have included income for the trust and new jobs, job training, and income for crofters and their families. The record makes it clear none of this would have happened under Vestey ownership.

As this is written, the Scottish Parliament is debating land reform. The achievement of the Assynt Crofters' Trust and similar buyouts that followed are much in mind. It remains to be seen whether the result of reform will be to continue tuning the old engine or a new approach to opportunities for community land ownership in the Highlands.

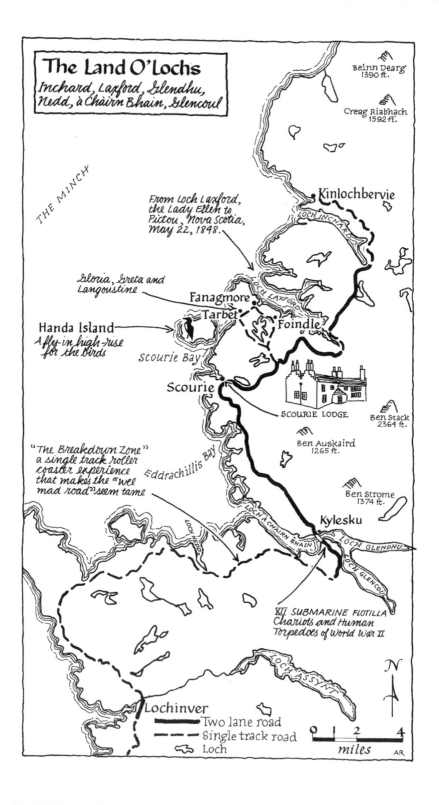

The Land O'Lochs
Inchard, Laxford, Glendhu, Nedd, à Chàirn Bhain, Glencoul

Beinn Dearg
1390 ft.

Creag Riabhach
1592 ft.

THE MINCH

Kinlochbervie

LOCH INCHARD

From Loch Laxford,
the Lady Ellen to
Pictou, Nova Scotia,
May 22, 1848.

LOCH LAXFORD

Gloria, Greta and
Langoustine

Fanagmore
Tarbet
Foindle

Handa Island
*A fly-in high-rise
for the birds*

Scourie Bay

Scourie

SCOURIE LODGE

Ben Stack
2364 ft.

Ben Auskaird
1265 ft.

"The Breakdown Zone"
*a single track roller
coaster experience
that makes the "wee
mad road" seem tame*

Eddrachillis Bay

Ben Strome
1374 ft.

LOCH NEDD

LOCH À CHÀIRN BHAIN

Kylesku

LOCH GLENDHU

LOCH GLENCOUL

XII SUBMARINE FLOTILLA
*Chariots and Human
Torpedoes of World War II*

LOCH ASSYNT

Lochinver

N

Two lane road
Single track road
Loch

0   2   4
miles

AR

CHAPTER SEVEN

SUBMARINES, HANDA, AND FOINDLE

CHE BELLA PANORAMA

YEARS AGO ON A trip to Italy, *che bella panorama* was one of the first phrases I mastered. And now here we were in the North West Highlands looking out at a place an exuberant copywriter might well describe as having a "pulse-pounding perspective" or views of "wrenching dimension."

To the northwest we could see the blue-gray surface of Loch Nedd, with low grass-green hills rising gently from loch shores, more newborn lambs, and beyond, whitecaps of Edrachillis Bay. When we turned around there was Abhainn Gileainn Leireag, a fertile river valley connecting Loch Nedd to Loch an Leothaid, and as a backdrop, peaks of the Quinag chain—Sail Gorm, Sail Gharbh, and Spidean Coinich—trailing off into the distance.

Che bella panorama!

The view did little to prepare me for a new driving experience, a single-track roller coaster—up to five hundred feet, down to eighty, up to four hundred, down to sixty—and so it went until the road deadheaded at the A894, a two-lane Highland superhighway that took us into Kylesku (**Kyle** skew). This is where the Assynt territory of Clan MacLeod ends and Sutherland, Duthaich mhic Aoidh, the

"Country of Mackay," begins. It is marked by the meeting of three great lochs—Loch Glendhu and Loch Glencoul, both freshwater lochs, and Loch a Chairn Bhain, a sea loch.

We stopped for lunch at the Kylesku Hotel, perched at water's edge just above the old ferry slip where the Maid of Glencoul once ferried cars across the loch. The first "ferry," a rowboat, dates back to the early 1800s, when herdsmen rode and cattle swam across on their way to market. The first car ferry went into service more than eighty years ago in 1920, and in 1975 the Maid of Glencoul, a roll-on-roll-off, was the first ferry able to handle large trucks. In 1984 the old Maid gave way to a graceful curving bridge, allowing drivers to speed across the lochs, going from Assynt to Sutherland with nary a pause.

A Different Kind of Chariot

The Barman at the Kylesku Hotel remembered when long waits for the ferry on a hot summer's day did wonders for bar business. He said the bridge is great for Highland commerce and fast connection between the north and Inverness and beyond, but he lamented the change of pace and fading memories. He encouraged us to stop at a small monument on the north shore erected as a memorial to the remarkable men of the XII Submarine Flotilla. We learned the flotilla was a unit of Midget Submarines (known as X-Craft) and Human Torpedoes (called Chariots) that trained in "these wild and beautiful waters" more than half a century ago in World War II. The Twelfth was one of the most decorated units of the armed forces. It was an all-volunteer unit with a long roll call of men who never returned from their heroic missions—ordinary seaman R. Anderson, sublieutenant K. V. F. Harris, stoker R. W. Pridhaus, lieutenant S. F. Stretton-Smith, leading seaman B. Trevethian. On and on went this list of men who fought the "good war."

Imagine, if you can, you are a Chariot driver, sitting underwater with your partner astride a battery-powered, twenty-foot-long, cold steel, torpedo-shaped hull with a six-hundred-pound explosive charge forming its nose. Your maximum speed is four miles per hour, and your battery has enough juice for a four-hour ride. Your breathing equipment is rudimentary even by 1943 standards, and your wet suit is known as "Clammy Death." On a moonless night a mother ship tows your Chariot in as close as possible to a protected enemy harbor, and then you are on your own, cutting your way through steel mesh sub nets, skirting mine fields, and attaching the explosive charge from the bow of your Chariot to the hull of the enemy ship. You set the timer and get the hell away, most likely to the shore, because your Chariot doesn't have enough power left to get you back to the mother ship. You are now in enemy territory, and the odds are in favor of the Germans capturing you before the resistance can save you.

In a four-man midget submarine (commander, engineer, seaman, diver), you are also towed in and cast off to cut sub nets and evade mines. Then, if you are the diver, you leave the sub through a diving compartment, swim underwater with a load of magnetic limpet mines, and attach them to the hull of an enemy ship. On 22 September 1943 in Tromso Fjord on the Norwegian coast, midget subs X-6 and X-7 did this kind of job on the battleship Tirpitz, a German floating fortress with eight fifteen-inch guns that had been hell on North Sea convoys. Divers from the two-thousand-ton subs X-6 and X-7 planted explosive charges on the bottom of the anchored 42,900-ton Tirpitz, disabling her turbines, propeller shafts, and rudder. This was the first step in keeping the battleship out of action. Torpedo planes finished the job. Above the Waves, a film made in 1956 starring John Mills, dramatized the story of the heroic assault of two midget subs, X-6 and X-7, on the battleship Tirpitz.

GETTINGTHEREITIS, THE DRIVER'S MALADY

I REALIZE NOW THAT as we sped along from Kylesku to Scourie (Skowry) at sixty miles an hour, I was in the grips of "Gettingthereitis," a driver's malady transmitted by bands of concrete with white lines down the middle designed by engineers for the most direct and efficient travel between two locations.

In contrast, single-track roads follow natural contours of the land, usually along routes of old cart trails. They have no clearly defined edge, tending to ease off into the country they cross. Road surfaces may be gravel or some other packed material, or even well-worn asphalt here and there where the local council had some money it had to spend before the end of the year. Sheep and lambs and the odd shaggy Highland cow graze on the verge with nary a look as you drift on by. Driving along, you have a sense of being connected to the lakes, moors, and marshes the single track wanders through. The message is "Hey, stop if you like, take a look, stroll about." You can almost hear the voice of poet William Henry Davies:

> What is this life if, full of care,
> We have no time to stand and stare

Concrete highways don't draw you on just because engineers and road builders have made it easier to go faster. Highways focus you on the road ahead because clearly defined edges create a dividing line between you and what's around. You become at best an observer of your surroundings, not a participant. Stopping for a long look at a peaceful loch now requires a conscious effort rather than the pleasure of a happening. And having to find a place to pull off is just one more problem. And so it was in those ten miles from Kylesku to Scourie.

An Island for the Birds

I KNEW SCOURIE WAS in the warming path of the Gulf Stream and had the most northerly palm trees in the world. In daydreams I saw luxuriant palms swaying gently in a soft breeze in the garden of Scourie Lodge, like something out of a Dorothy Lamour movie. Reality was something else. The breeze was more Arctic than Aegean, and palm trees consisted of a tight cluster of seven shaggy New Zealand cabbage palms, grown from seeds sent by New Zealand relatives to a Lodge gardener 150 years before. Scourie Lodge, all white with a light gray trim and eight chimneys, sits elegantly on a hillside looking out over Scourie Bay. The Duke of Sutherland (of the million acre Sutherlands) built it for his bride in 1835. Later the lodge was home for Evander MacIver, Sutherland's factor (manager), who was remembered for harsh clearances and high rents. After various other incarnations, including a period of near ruin, the lodge was transformed into a comfortable, well-kept bed-and-breakfast by Penny Hawker.

Paul Theroux, writing about his travel experiences and taking advantage of opportunities, quotes a line from Shakespeare, "All is readiness." Put another way, serendipity doesn't find you. It occurs more often than not because you are ready for what comes your way. And so it was that our Handa Island experience became very personal and very special.

Handa Island is a world-class sanctuary for seabirds and is administered by the Scottish Wildlife Trust. Visiting Handa was our main reason for stopping off in Scourie, but there was a problem. The regular ferry to Handa leaves from nearby Tarbet and lets you off on the island for a two- or three-hour walkabout. First of all, this Creaky Traveler and creaky G are in no way equipped for a four-mile jaunt where "the terrain is rough, the cliffs are steep, and the weather can change quickly, so take care." Also, I really wanted to see the nesting cliffs up close from the sea. It all fell into place. The tiny Scourie Pier was just down the hill from the Lodge, and Penny knew Ken Nash, a boatman who could run us out to the cliffs in his "cruiser." The next morning we met Ken, a burly, naturally happy type, at the pier. His cruiser was to boats what single track roads are to highways—slow, small, low to the water, given to the odd spray of salt water, and in tune with its surroundings.

Handa Island, sitting in isolation in Scourie Bay about two-and-half miles from the pier, is a massive, mile-square hunk of red-hued Torridonian sandstone with cliffs rising vertically to heights of four hundred feet, topped with moorland and lochans. In the early nine-teenth century a somewhat eccentric "kingdom" of twelve crofting families shared Handa with seabirds, subsisting on the birds, fish, and an annual potato crop. They had their own "parliament" consisting of all married males who met each morning to deal with the day's busi-ness and a "queen" who was the oldest widow on the island. (I wonder if they thought the oldest widow was chosen by divine intervention.)

Handa served two other purposes. Mainlanders buried their dead on Handa because bodies buried on the mainland tended to be dug up by marauding wolves. Also, enterprising mainland crofters rowed their sheep and cattle across for summer pasture. The potato famine of 1846 forced the twelve families to leave the island. Some stayed in the Highlands, and others migrated to Cape Breton in Canada—which must have felt like home, except for the fact that they didn't have their own parliament or queen. And so Handa was left to the birds.

As we approached Handa, from a distance the Great Stack appeared as a monolith erupting from the sea and coming forward to meet us. As we came closer, we could see the results of thousands of years of weathering of the sandstone—horizontal layers serving as residential floors in this towering, multistory, avian high-rise. It is especially towering when your perspective is looking nearly straight up from a small boat bobbing at the bottom. Nature performed another design feat in a cleavage between two sections of the rock face. Beginning fifteen feet above the sea, wind and water created a stage forty feet wide and twenty feet deep and carved a monumental proscenium arch rising fifty feet above the stage. All this is "painted" in subtle hues of gray, red, purple, brown, and green. Moving about on the stage and walking proudly upright was a cast of about thirty white-breasted razorbills that look and walk like miniature penguins. Then the light drizzle stopped. The sun came out and everything glistened. What a performance.

The horizontal layers of the Great Stack provide ideal, disturbance-free places for seabirds to breed. According to Andre Romskorf, a local authority, many of Handa's 180,000 seabirds live for twenty years or more and return to exactly the same spot on the same floor of the cliff year after year. In this seabird city each pair holds a territory of a few square feet, except for guillemots, which go in for communal living. There is a strict hierarchy of neighborhoods in bird city for the principal tenants.

- Fulmars nest on narrow ledges near the very top of the cliff. Theirs is a one-chick family. The male and female take turns of two to five days over eight weeks to brood their single egg.

- Guillemots and razorbills, members of the auk family, roost on the floors immediately below the fulmars. Razorbills are also single-chick families and lay their one egg in crevices. Guillemots are an altogether different story. They have a liberated lifestyle, nesting in packed communities and sharing mates, eggs, and responsibility for chicks. G and I were really sorry we weren't around to see the guillemots push their chicks off the ledges for their first attempt at flight and their first swim. This takes place at about twenty days, nearly forty days before true fledging. As Malcolm Ogilvie reports the event in Birds of Britain, "It is a remarkable sight as the half-grown chicks, accompanied by a parent, flutter frantically on stubby wings gliding steeply down, to a belly-flop landing on the water below." That's it for a comfortable life as chicks on the cliff. Now they are seabirds.

- Kittiwakes are on the next level down. On narrow ledges, they build nests made of grass bound together by droppings. They are true ocean gulls who come ashore only to breed and then spend the rest of the year, including winter, at sea.

We were able to see and study the fulmars, guillemots, razorbills, and kittiwakes. There may well have been other birds we did not recognize and some that had not yet arrived. For readers who are birders, I will complete the list of Handa visitors. Puffins nest in burrows on top of the cliffs. Arctic and great skuas are powerful birds that occupy the moorland and bully other birds, forcing them to disgorge fish. Skuas also steal eggs and chicks from kittiwake nests. Red throated divers raise young on the lochans, oystercatchers and ringed plovers nest on the beaches, and barnacle geese winter over on the island. There are also shags, terns, gulls, and auks in this ornithological paradise.

With stiff necks and no more film, we headed back to the mainland and a welcome cup of tea at Scourie Lodge. Our journey to Handa Island turned out to be one of those rare adventures when a number of quite wonderful pieces come together to make $2+2=5$. The small boat in a big sea creating a sense of voyage to parts unknown, the mass of Handa rising from the sea and morphing into this colorful tower of sandstone terraces filled with thousands of raucous breeding seabirds in their infinite variety, the razorbill performance on nature's sunlit stage—and all this just for the two of us.

GLORIA AND GRETA

TARBET IS A TOTAL contrast to Handa Island. Handa is a huge seabird action theater with much motion and loud bird talk. Tarbet is small, silent, and moody, a stage set designed for a dramatic final curtain.

The narrowest of narrow tracks leads to Tarbet. It follows a tiny stream that wanders through a valley beginning at Loch a Bragh Ghainmhch near the Claisfearn Burnt Mound and empties into Loch nam Brac. There the water spreads into glens and hollows, giving the Loch the shape of a jigsaw piece with a half-dozen necks and heads. Patches of pasture and a few thin Highland cattle looking as if they have been through hell border the track, with hills on both sides rising to three hundred and four hundred feet. There is a bull warning sign, but no bull. After Loch nam Brac the track moves up steeply on a twenty-percent grade, and at the top of the hill there is Tarbet below at the northern end of the Sound of Handa—a cove the map identifies with what may be more than a touch of exaggeration as the Port of Tarbet.

Southwest, about a mile across the sound, is the great hulk of Handa Island, due west the small island of Eilean an Aigeich, and to the north Sgeirean Glase, a cluster of eleven tiny islands—the first one nearly touching the Tarbet cove. These islands are not anything like the small, placid-looking green mounds of the Summer Isles off Achiltibue that gave us a sense of contented timelessness. These islands and the mainland shore are rough-hewn products of the Ice Age and Atlantic gales—raw, intricate stretches of rock (skerries) besieged by the sea in winter storms. Even on the calm days we were there, waves crashing into rocky inlets spouted towers of spray.

For the rest of the scene, imagine dark clouds in the distance behind these somber islands, some silhouetted where the sun breaks through, others framed with crimson. The light continues to change as the sun sets, slowly improving the scene by the moment. On the golden sand of the beach, beginning back from the shore, a gracefully curving stone walk with a flimsy rusting iron railing disappears into the sea. I shut my eyes. Was it Gloria Swanson or Greta Garbo? Yes, it was Garbo— dressed in a diaphanous gown, around her neck a filmy scarf lifted by a gentle breeze, walking gracefully, slowly down the stone walk, her hand on the railing as if seeking support (will she or won't she?). Then with only a wistful look back, waves breaking at her knees and then her waist, Garbo walked into the sea and the sunset. The end.

Nephrops Norvegicus

It was getting on into the evening, and my vision began shifting from Garbo to wild salmon leaping into a frying pan. At Tarbet cove we were steps from the Seafood Café, the only building in sight. It was top-rated by Scotland the Best! which described it as, "A charming conservatory restaurant . . . Julian catches your seafood from his boat and Jackie [wife] cooks it." There were just a few glitches: this was the first night of the season the café was open; we were the only guests; the view was great, but the charm was somewhat diluted by the ten wooden picnic tables with picnic benches all neatly lined up in a row; and Julian was harvesting only langoustine from his boat this time of year.

I went for the fish and chips, G for the langoustine. They arrived in battle order, a platoon of twelve of these stunted lobsters arranged artistically around the rim of a large platter, facing out in full-armored regalia, claws at the ready, black beady eyes protruding on stalks, glistening, and daring G to try and get at their meaty innards. G doesn't much like peeling shells off cooked shrimp, and the best that can be said for her performance was that she fought the langoustine to a draw.

Langoustine are of the species *nephrops norvegicus* and are also referred to in the Highlands as Norway lobster or Dublin Bay prawns, in Italy as scampo, and by some Scottish fishermen as whole prawns. The Fish Society of Scotland under Fish Code #8335 explains, "The shells of langoustine are much stronger than those of prawns. The best way to handle them is to press the undersides of shells inwards until the top part cracks, then peel away from the top." Let's just say G never quite mastered the art, and I doubt she will try again. The fish and chips were super, and the dessert of double chocolate was delicious.

FANAGMORE AND FOINDLE

FANAGMORE (**FAN** AK MORE) and Foindle (**Foyn** dal), along with Tarbet, have one home each and are testimony to the sparse population of Sutherland. Population per square mile in the United Kingdom is ninety, in Scotland twenty-six, in the Highlands three, and in Sutherland one.

Fanagmore is a mile northeast of Tarbet, and Foindle is a mile southeast of Fanagmore. You cannot get to Foindle without going by Fanagmore, which was great because it was probably the sweetest and slowest drive we had on the entire trip. Ewes and lambs graze along roads all over the Highlands and occasionally wander across the road. But there in Foindle the narrow track had become a lounge and nap area for the woollies who set no records for response time, meandering ever so slowly out of the way. Could this be the origin of the popular definition of "foindle"—"the art of queue jumping by gently meandering up along the line?"

Fanagmore and Foindle sit in their own small coves on the south shore of Loch Laxford, which local people argue is the most beautiful loch in the Highlands. This must have made departure by "cleared" families on sailing ships more than a century ago even more melancholy. The Duke of Sutherland chartered one of these boats, a three-masted, 380-ton bark, *Lady Ellen,* to ship tenants he was clearing from his lands in Sutherland and Assynt to Canada. The *Lady Ellen* departed from Loch Laxford on 22 May 1848 with 158 men, women, and children in its cramped hold, a space of about eighty feet by twenty feet. Their journey across the north Atlantic from Loch Laxford to landing in Pictou, Nova Scotia, took thirty-nine days.

According to records of the Immigrant Ships Transcriber Guild, there were seventy-eight males and eighty females on board, including an eighty-year-old widow Mrs. Ann Sutherland. Families named McLeod, McKay, McKenzie, and McIntosh accounted for nearly two-thirds of the 158 passengers, with Gunn, Falconer, Morrison, and Mathison making up most of the rest.

The first Scottish settlers, 189 in all, arrived at Pictou Harbor on 15 September 1773 aboard the Hector. Between then and 1849, a total of 120 ships carrying nearly twenty thousand Scots docked at Pictou. It was with good reason Pictou became known as New Scotland.

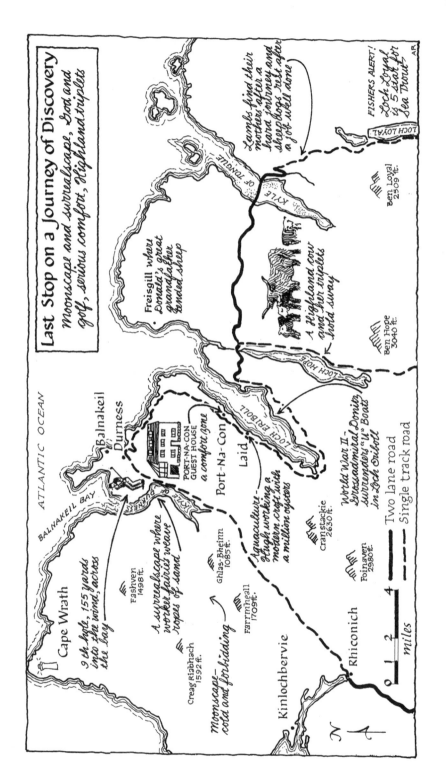

Last Stop on a Journey of Discovery

Moonscape and surrealscape, God and golf, serious comfort, Highland triplets

FISHERS ALERT!
Loch Loyal is 5 star for Sea Trout

Lambs find their mothers after a hard journey and a sheepdog's rest after a job well done

KYLE OF TONGUE

LOCH LOYAL

Ben Loyal
2509 ft.

Freisgill where Donald's great grandfather landed sheep

A Highland cow and her triplets hold sway

Ben Hope
3040 ft.

LOCH HOPE

ATLANTIC OCEAN

Balnakeil

Durness

LOCH ERIBOLL

PORT-NA-CON
GUEST HOUSE
a comfort zone

Port-Na-Con

BALNAKEIL BAY

A surrealscape where worker fairies weave ropes of sand

KYLE OF DURNESS

Laid

World War II-
Lütsosadmiral Dönitz
surrenders "U" Boats
in Loch Eriboll

Cape Wrath

9 th hole, 155 yards into the wind, across the bay

Fashven
1498 ft.

Ghlas-Bheinn
1085 ft.

Aquaculture-
Alugh working a
modern craft with
a million oysters

Cranstackie
2630 ft.

Moonscape-
cold and forbidding

Creag Riabhach
1592 ft.

Farrmheall
1709 ft.

Foinaven
2980 ft.

Kinlochbervie

Rhiconich

N

Two lane road
Single track road

0 1 2 4
miles

AR

CHAPTER EIGHT

LOCH ERIBOLL

FROM MOONSCAPE TO SURREALSCAPE

THE ROAD SHIFTS INLAND as you drive north from Scourie. At Rhiconich (Ree co neehh) it narrows to single track and begins to rise slowly through harsh, barren jumbles of rock and dull, gray bogs, more like a moonscape than a landscape. Occasional lochs and the three-thousand-foot peaks of Ceann Garbh and Garne Mor do little to soften the somber mood on this dark, drizzly day. I drive. G dozes.

Just past Loch Tarbhaidh, after reaching six hundred feet, the track begins a slow descent as it runs parallel to the river Dionard. We see two men in the slow, steady motions of digging and stacking peat. The river widens a bit, and in an instant we have left the moonscape and are the sole possessors of a surrealscape. A mile wide, deep blue, with green hills on the western shore, the Kyle of Durness flows nearly five miles to Balnakeil Bay (Bal na keel) and the Atlantic. Along the entire way the shallow sand bottom sculpted by wind and wave harmonizes with river water flowing out and tidal water coming in. This creates a wild pattern of swirls, crescents, and half moons, merging and changing on the water's surface.

The magic of the moment reminds me of a story told about the Kyle of Durness that I suspect is also told of other places where sand and water combine to such wondrous effect. The Witch of Tain Hill sent the chief of the Mackays a box of worker fairies to build a bridge across the Kyle. The messenger was told most emphatically not to open the box under any circumstances, but curiosity got the better of him. He opened the box and was immediately encircled by a hundred fairies, each yelling "obair, obair, obair," meaning "work, work, work." The messenger, in a moment of inspiration, set the fairies to weaving ropes of sand, an impossible task that could never be completed. The fairies are still there toiling away, and when the wind is right they can be heard lamenting their fate, never to go home again.

At Keodale another kind of ferry takes passengers to the west shore of the Kyle. From there a minibus carries them eleven miles through wilderness to Cape Wrath, the most northerly point on the British mainland, where another Stevenson lighthouse guards the coast from its rocky perch 317 feet above the sea. Nearby are Clo Mor Cliffs, the highest sheer sea cliffs in Britain, with a drop of 921 feet. The name "Wrath" doesn't come from the fury of the sea crashing against the rocks or the many ships that foundered there before the lighthouse was built, but from the Norse "hvarf," meaning "turning place." Viking galleys used the cape as a navigation point for guiding raids along the Scottish coast.

We decided not to invest the better part of a day on Cape Wrath, especially after we learned the area is closed on some days because it also serves as a bombing range. A brochure explained, "1,000-pound bombs may be dropped" as final training for fighter pilots "before being asked to perform in battle situations." And then there was the woman taking pictures at the cape who was lifted over the edge of a cliff by a gust of wind.

THE ESTIMABLE LESLEY BLACK

AT THE VILLAGE OF Durness and the most northerly ATM in mainland Britain, the track turns east for three miles along a string of Atlantic beaches, and from Respond Bay it runs south along the western shore of Loch Eriboll (Eh rib ol). Then it winds down a narrower track, past the crumbling stone walls of abandoned croft houses to Port-Na-Con Guest House and the estimable Lesley Black.

Lesley is ample, warm, remarkably energetic, and comfortable with herself, has a ready genuine smile, and does what she loves. Her apparel always included a snow-white bib apron that reminded me of the Buena Vista Grocery, the corner store in Detroit that got the Rovetch family through the Depression and on to better things. When working in the store, I also wore a white bib apron and waited on customers in the glow of my father's approval.

Lesley lived in north London and worked for fourteen years as an accountant for Her Majesty's Civil Service. Her husband Ken was with the Ministry of Defense for more than thirty years, working in quality assurance. Ken was up for retirement, Lesley had had it with London and the bureaucracy, and her dream of a guesthouse in the Highlands grew and grew. In 1991 she saw an ad for Port-Na-Con, which had been converted to a guesthouse in 1984. Lesley and Ken had found what they were looking for, and that was it, to our good fortune.

Let me try to define the special quality of Port-Na-Con. With apologies to Gertrude Stein, a Holiday Inn is a Holiday Inn is a Holiday Inn, all stamped from the same mold. Port-Na-Con is a one-of-a-kind, very personal expression of Lesley. It is comfortable, very comfortable. The rooms are neat, not fussy, with good mattresses and excellent bedside reading lights—comfortable. The food is not showy and has no esoteric glazes or sauces but is fresh from garden and sea, nicely prepared, and satisfying. In a word—comfortable.

A newly built conservatory has windows all round with views north to the Atlantic, east to green fields against gray limestone hills across the loch, and south to the dark peaks of Ben Hope and Ben Loyal. It is an inviting, comfortable, "do what you will" kind of space for an afternoon read and cup of tea, watching otters do acrobatics near the shore, or as often as not, a little drowse. But there is always a dram of the best before dinner. The other guests, Donald Grant and newly married Duncan and Pat Gifillan, had been to Port-Na-Con before, and, you will not be surprised to learn, we found them very comfortable company.

It's a Long Way to Al na Callich

Donald's forbears came from the east side of Loch Eriboll, and he comes to Port-Na-Con each year to research a bit more on his family. His searches have taken him through historic records—birth, baptism, marriage, death, burial—plus talks with older relatives (the recollections of one eighty-year-old took him back 150 years) and family papers including a will, letters, and a collection of postcards saved by a cousin in Edwardian times. Donald's great-grandfather was one of the last shepherds to tend flocks in Freisgill (Freesh gill), a fierce spot at the head of Loch Eriboll open to winter gales blowing in from the North Atlantic. Even today Freisgill, while marked on the Ordnance Survey, is three miles from the nearest track or road.

Donald told me that when his great-grandmother died on Hogmanay (New Years Eve, 1887), it took several days to carry her to her burial place from the isolated pasture area of Freisgill, first by litter, then by boat on Loch Eriboll and another boat on Loch Hope, and finally by a two-wheel cart to a tiny cemetery at Al na Callich (a sweet spot south of Ben Hope). She lies there beside her parents and infant daughter. As G and I drove by the cemetery on our meanderings, I tipped my hat (metaphorically) to Donald's great-grandmother.

Port-Na-Con was built more than two hundred years ago at water's edge as a customhouse and harbor store. The total population then was over a thousand (now around three hundred), and most goods came in once a month on the St. Ola, a steamship from Aberdeen. It was 1939 before serviceable roads connected Durness with the rest of the Highlands. Another measure of its remoteness is that the village of Durness did not have central electricity or a public water and sewer system until 1955. By then it had come a long way from what the local minister, Reverend William Findlater, found in 1834:

> The natives are generally lively in their dispositions, social in their habits, although it cannot be said they are remarkable for their cleanliness, cattle and people using the same shelters.

When engaged in labour either at sea or on land they endure a great deal of fatigue. Spending evenings in each other's houses in the plentiful hamlets sharing the news of the country, repeating the songs of their native bard or listening to legendary tales. All natives speak Gaelic, a proportion of the young can speak English. The habits of dram drinking, acquired by both sexes in the course of their mixing together have tended to deteriorate the morals of the people considerably. Their attendance at religious ordinances, however, is pretty regular.

At the time of Reverend Findlater's observation, the population of the Durness Parish in 1834 was 1,180, including 206 families, most living in "scattered tiny clachans [hamlets] in huts of turf or dry stone, plastered on the inside with clay. They raised black cattle and goats, grew potatoes and inferior oats, used their wooden plough to break the earth, brewed rough beer and distilled raw whiskey." Population pressure on poor land and primitive agricultural practices had been growing. "Higher numbers of children were surviving thanks to Dr. Dunnet from Thurso, who had started inoculating for smallpox."

Between the clearances, forced moves to crofting townships, emigration overseas, and the search for jobs elsewhere, population of the Durness Parish went into a steady decline—870 in 1901, 413 in 1951, and 338 in 1981. By 1997, with the introduction of fish farming and increased tourism, the population had grown to 350 people living in 150 households in surviving crofting townships strung out along the coast—Durine, Balvolich, Balnakeil, Sanobeg, Lerinmore, Lerinbeg, Smoo, and Sangomore. Recently a fish farm in Loch Eriboll shut down with a loss of ten jobs, an economic disaster for the area and a measure of the scale required for thinking in terms of the North West Highlands.

Locals recall with great satisfaction when German U-boats surrendered to the British Twenty-First Escort Group in Loch Eriboll.

SURRENDER: GROSSADMIRAL KARL DONITZ

MAY 4TH 1945 SIGNAL. ATTENTION: ALL U-BOATS. CEASE-FIRE AT ONCE. STOP ALL HOSTILE ACTION AGAINST ALLIED SHIPPING. DONITZ

Instructions from Grossadmiral Karl Donitz follow. ANNEX-URE "A": SURRENDER OF GERMAN "U" BOAT FLEET. To all "U" Boats at sea: Carry out the following instructions forthwith: (A) Surface immediately and remain surfaced. (B) Report immediately your position. (C) Fly a large black flag by day. (D) Burn navigation lights by night. (E) Jettison all ammunition, remove breachblocks from guns and render torpedoes safe by removing pistols. All mines are to be rendered safe. (F) Make all signals in P/F. (G) Follow strictly the instructions for proceeding to Allied ports. (H) Observe strictly the orders of Allied Representatives to refrain from scuttling or in any way damaging your "U" Boat. ANNEXURE "B": Area "A": Join one of the following routes [details given] and proceed along it to Loch Eriboll.

Between May 10th and May 15th, 1945, one-by-one, black flags of defeat flying from conning towers, the pride of the North Atlantic wolfpack, twelve German subs came to heel in Loch Eriboll, surrendering to the British 21st Escort Group. One of the subs, Number 1105, a type VII-C named the "Black Panther," had sunk the HMS Redmill, a destroyer of the 21st Group, just weeks before. The Black Panther was experimental, coated with synthetic rubber to counter Allied sub-finding sonar devices. Number 1105 was delivered to the U.S. navy to research the anti-sonar process and now serves a peaceful purpose as part of a fish reef off the New England coast.

THRUST TECTONICS—TWO PERSPECTIVES

WHILE MOST LOCHS OFFER a sense of protection from the open sea, it was clear as we drove along the shore of Loch Eriboll that it is more an extension of the sea—ten miles north to south and four miles across in places, and ninety to 360 feet deep. G looked at the eastern and southern shores of the loch with her artist's eye and saw rock formations that are extraordinary in their variety, color, and texture. Geologists look at the same scene and see a world-class research site in structural geology and mountain building. They rhapsodize over Loch Eriboll's "geometry of thrust surfaces"—crushing, overlapping, layering, folding, and bending caused by compression in the earth's crust. In geospeak, the combination of imbrication, deformation, shear strain, and bed-parallel shortening has produced a "3-D exposure of thrust system architecture" in a "site internationally important for understanding thrust tectonics." According to Webster, thrust tectonics are compressive strains in the crust of the earth that produce reverse or thrust faults.

A group with commercial interests has looked at this topography and seen money squeezing out of these same rocks. As reported in the press, "faceless, negligent, absentee landlord," Vibel SA, offshore (Liechtenstein) owner of the 9,400-acre Durness Estate, has been lobbying for years to build a superquarry. The purpose would be to extract and crush five million tons or more a year of rock (granite, gneiss, compacted limestone, and sandstone) for roads and building material. A marine terminal would need to be built on Loch Eriboll to ship the crushed rock, mostly to Europe. Locals and Scottish environmental groups oppose the plan because it would destroy the environment and opportunities for tourism. According to a recent government study, tourism "will underpin the [Sutherland] economy, not a quarry development." Even with this advice on the table, the sound of rocks and money can still be heard.

The Vibel Durness Estate includes Laid, a township of eighteen crofts scattered along the rugged, rocky, western shore of Loch Eriboll just south of Port-Na-Con. The Laid Common Grazing Committee has been trying for several years to buy three thousand acres of common grazing from the Durness Estate as part of a boot-strap plan to bring Laid back to "full life." Laid was established in the 1830s for tenants "cleared" from the hamlets of Eriboll and Strathbeg on the fertile, lime-rich east shore of the loch. In 1993 only three resident tenants remained on Laid crofts. By 2000 the number was back up to seven. We drove through Laid several times on our meanderings.

One of the seven tenants is Hugh Maclellan, whose forbears were among the families "cleared" to Laid. Hugh traces his family back almost fifteen hundred years to Clan Gunn and clan chief George the Crowner. Hugh's grandmother, Catherine McKay, wrote in her reminiscences, *Down Memory Lane*, about the life of her family and other crofters in Laid:

> The people who were evicted [cleared] to Laid had great difficulty in clearing from the stony, heather-covered small patches of ground, digging with spades, in which to grow small quantities of potatoes, oats and vegetables for food. But despite difficulties and hardships the evicted lived long lives in Laid. . . . Each crofter had one or two sheep and the wool was spun on spinning wheels into yard and knitted into garments, or taken to a weaver in Durness to be made into cloth. . . .When the sea was out [the sheep] made their way to the shore to eat seaweed. . . . In spring shoals of herring came into Loch Eriboll. These were caught in nets and salted in wooden barrels. They were eaten for mid-day meals with potatoes. . . . Hens were kept, most crofters had a cow. . . . A wedding was a great event. Headed by a piper, the guests marched to the school in couples from the bride's home and then returned there for dinner, followed by a dance. The children waited at the roadside for handfuls of pennies thrown to them.

More recently, in 1940, Hugh's grandfather was one of the heroes of Dunkirk. In his small Loch Eriboll lobster boat, he braved the English Channel, along with hundreds of other owners of small craft, who, under enemy fire, rescued thousands of British soldiers pinned down on the beaches at Dunkirk.

Hugh returned to the family croft in 1994, after a career in the merchant navy, to raise his two children and launch a mix of modern croft-based businesses—bed-and-breakfasts, aquaculture (a million oysters in Loch Eriboll at the foot of his croft), and forestry, planting native species of types that once covered nearby hills. As clerk (elected chairman) of the Laid Common Grazing Committee, he is in the middle of the land reform battle. Hugh says land reform legislation before the Scottish Parliament may yet give the Laid Common Grazing Committee a chance to buy the Vibel land. They need it to move ahead with a heritage trail they believe will boost tourism and take other steps to preserve the rural character of the area. If the land reform bill does pass, Lesley Black, who is Grazing Committee secretary, explained just how daunting buying the land will be. To begin with, agreement will be required by fifty percent of residents on the election rolls and then by fifty percent of all resident crofters. This is followed by a government feasibility study, recommendation to proceed, and setting the proper purchase price. At that point Laid could qualify for the "lolly" (money), a ninety-five-percent purchase grant from the Scottish Land Fund.

LADS O' PAIRTS

I LEARNED FROM HUGH that his great-grandmother and grandmother both taught school in Laid in a span of time from the late 1800s to 1932. This was a period when "public" education grew to include subscription schools (7.5 pence a quarter for reading and writing, ten pence for Latin and arithmetic), side schools ("school" sheds on wheels towed to remote areas), and church schools. By 1900 ten side schools were affiliated with the "proper school" at Laid. There was near-universal primary education in Scotland and the belief that able boys, "lads o' pairts," no matter how humble their background, could rise to the top with hard work and their own talent.

A good part of my professional life has been spent working to improve schools. I wanted to talk to kids and teachers at Durness Primary School and see a school where total enrollment was about the same size as a single class in schools I knew. So on an overcast afternoon, I visited bright and cheery Durness Primary. One thing became clear. The Scots back up their belief in "lads (and now girls too) o' pairts" with an impressive array of resources.

Enrollment at Durness Primary is thirty children, ages four through eleven, grouped in two classrooms, grades one through three and four through seven. Staff includes two full-time teachers plus six visiting teachers and specialists for music, art, physical education, developmental needs, speech therapy (four students), and a deaf boy. All the kids in his class are learning sign language. There is also a tutor for five kids studying bagpipes, an auxiliary classroom teacher, a cook, a cleaner, and a school secretary. Gaelic and French are taught "in addition to the usual subjects," and there is a darkroom because "the school does a lot of photography work." Head teacher Graham Bruce is given one day off from teaching every two weeks for "management tasks."

I talked with the kids in Bruce's classroom—where computers and wall art were much in evidence—about which subjects they liked best and how high the Rocky Mountains were compared to mountains near Durness. Then it was recess time, and the kids dashed for the playground. Bruce and his students had an easy relationship. As Bruce said, "Being together in the same classroom for four years, we really get to know each other." Hugh MacLellan's daughter Julie had been in Bruce's class. Now Julie and her brother Michael go to Kinlochbervie High School, which is twenty miles south of Durness and has ninety-seven students in grades eight through thirteen, nine full-time teachers, and eight part-time teachers.

KHS opened in 1995. If Julie and Michael had gone to high school before 1995, they would have had to travel seventy miles to the east coast of the Highlands, gone to school in Golspie, and been boarded in a hostel. Then every day on their way to school they could have looked up at the hundred-foot-high monument to the First Duke of Sutherland (erected by "a mourning and grateful tenantry [to] a judicious, kind and liberal landlord.") atop 1,300-foot Beinn a' Bhragaidh and thought about this "kind" man who had so cruelly cleared their forbears from fertile lands to make way for sheep.

Pheasants and Triplets Hold Sway

With Ben Hope as a 3,040-foot backdrop to the half moon south shore of Loch Eriboll, we continued our drive past Laid, around the southern end of the loch and up the eastern shore, stopping for a look at the Ard Neakie Lime Kilns. These giant stone kilns were built in 1870 on a hammerhead promontory, Geodh' an Sqadain. The kilns, constructed of local stone, are fifty feet high and about a hundred feet across where they face the edge of the loch. At the rear, the kilns are fitted in a cliff so limestone and coke could be shoveled in from the road above. Limestone was mined from a quarry next to the kiln, and coke was brought in by sea to a pier at the foot of the kiln. The coke and lime mixture was burned, and the resulting "quick-lime" carted away to farms and crofts. Nearby we passed Wally, a life-sized, fiberglass killer whale that scares seals away from fish farms dotted along the bays and coves of Loch Eriboll.

There was something appropriate about this juxtaposition of Wally, hard at work at today's tasks, with the abandoned nineteenth-century lime kilns in the background.

Aquaculture, including oyster and mussel farming, is seen in the Loch Eriboll Aquaculture Framework Plan as providing "innovative economic opportunities and jobs" along inshore waters while striking "a balance between the need for sustainable economic development and safeguard on the natural heritage interest" in this area where population density is "less than one person per square kilometer." The aquaculture plan was developed by the Highland Council in consultation with local commercial and recreation users of the loch. As noted above, in another show of the left hand not knowing what the right hand is doing, the Highland Council has kept the superquarry option in its ten-year economic development plan for Loch Eriboll.

Further north on the eastern shore of Loch Eriboll, the single track turns sharply east across the top of the Highlands and reverts to a concrete highway. After a few miles, at the hamlet of Hope, the highway continues on and an "unclassified road," something between a wide path and a narrow track, runs due south along the eastern shore of Loch Hope. It is obviously an area where a good bit of the quick-lime went. Beside the track and on the other side of bluest of blue Loch Hope, verdant fields were rich with masses of ferns and clumps of willows and birches. It wouldn't have come as a surprise if Puck and other mischievous elves and fairies had come swinging out of the trees, sung a happy tune, and danced among the ferns.

Instead of elves and fairies, eight proud and beautiful pheasants occupied the narrow track. Neither offended nor concerned by our presence, they showed no inclination to yield the right of way. They dillied and they dallied, and finally, one by one, they decided to waddle off into the bushes.

On our way again, and just about as I was to shift up into the second of five gears, strolling out of the brush onto the track came the largest, shaggiest, biggest-horned, most mellow-eyed Highland cow the world has ever seen. She seemed a more-than-adequate companion for Paul Bunyan and his Ox, Babe. Then, just after we had gotten used to this beast staring in the window of our car, out from the bushes came one, then two, and finally the third of her triplet calves. They, too, were headed south along the track. We followed mother's swaying butt and udders, driving slowly at a discreet distance for about half an hour, when she finally led her brood off the track and on to greener pastures.

OF FISHERS AND LAMBS

AT THE BOTTOM OF Loch Hope the track continued, trailing now
along the upper ledge of Strath More. The river Strath, a wide stripe
of deep blue with green borders, gently winds along at the floor of
the grayish-brown, bracken-covered valley. After a series of sweeping
bends in the track, we headed north along the base of Ben Loyal with
Loch Loyal on our right. Loch Eriboll is raw. Loch Hope is pretty.
Loch Loyal is best defined as charming. Small clusters of birches and
willows are perched on rocky promontories along the loch shore,
hanging over blue-gray water, with the hills of Beinn Stumanadh on
guard in the background.

There we came across yet another variety of outdoor life—three
green Land Rovers and six fisherpersons, each properly decked out in
hip-length waders, many-pocketed fishing vests, hats with a fishing
fly or two in the band (Hairy Mary for salmon and Dazzle for trout),
and elegant long casting rods. For each two fishers, there was one
attentive "Ghillie." These guides show them, at around a hundred dollars each for four or five hours, where and how to fish on a section of
the loch where all riparian rights to salmon fishing are privately
owned. Laws regulate how, when, and by whom salmon may be
caught. Trout pretty much have to look out for themselves.

Clearly these fishers were in the right place. Four and a half miles
long and one mile wide, Loch Loyal is rated five stars for sea trout and
a bit less for brown trout and salmon. Sea trout are migratory and are
called steelhead, an endangered species in the United States. Oliver
Fuller of Strathbeg, said to be wisest among the wise when it comes
to fishing, writes that sea trout "fight furiously and are well worth the
antisocial hours necessary in their capture. Tactics employed are usually night or very early morning with small bright flies fished on the
surface." As for Atlantic salmon, they begin "in a gravel bed in a
Highland burn perhaps thousands of feet up in the mountains to the
river proper and then to sea to feed and grow off Greenland. Then
returning through armies of predators to their place of birth to spawn

a new generation." In Scotland, as in the United States, there are serious arguments about the declining number of returning wild salmon
caused by breeding practices, waste, pollution, and diseases on
salmon farms.

A little after we passed the fishing party the heavens opened to a
heavy dose of Highland dew. I hoped the fishers shared Gerard
Manley Hopkins' poetic feelings on wet and wildness in his poem
"Inversnaid."

> *What would the world be, once bereft*
> *Of wet and wildness? Let them be left,*
> *O let them be left, wildness and wet;*
> *Long live the weeds and the wilderness yet.*

But then changeable Highland weather produced a sunlit evening
in time for us to fall in behind a "roadfull" of lambs, hundreds of them
trying to catch up with their mothers who had forged ahead, seeming
to know their destination was a richer pasture. First there were pheasants, then big mama and triplets, then six fishers, and finally sheep
dogs barking, lambs crying for mothers, mothers crying for their
babies, and us creeping along behind. After a half hour or so the flock
got to its new pasture, and the ewes went quite happily to serious
grazing. Because of their short legs, the baby lambs had fallen far to
the rear in the forced march and were now in a wild frenzy of calling
and dashing about to find their mothers. In the miraculous way nature
has of bonding mother to child by sound and smell, the flock ultimately
got sorted out. And there before us was this bright green pasture full of
ewes and lambs, with each and every lamb nursing happily, head under,
knees down, rear end up, and tail wagging fast and furiously in pure
joy. I thought of the wind power waiting to be captured. G, ever
maternal, was saddened, having just seen all those lost baby lambs
crying out in desperate longing for their mothers.

The shepherd and his dogs surveyed their work with some satisfaction. We chatted with the shepherd and learned, among other things,

that he had taken his two kids to Disney World in Florida and visited relatives in the States the year before. This was no surprise. The shepherd was the fifth among farmers, barkeeps, and workmen we had met who had recently been to Orlando and visited relatives. It was the same in Ireland when we barged down the river Barrow. All the lockkeepers had taken their families to Disney World in Florida and visited relatives. Other common vacation choices seemed to be the Canaries, Spain, or the south of France. Workers of the world have united.

BALNAKEIL CRAFT VILLAGE—LIVING UGLY

ON OUR WAY TO Balnakeil Church (at the same site where St. Maelrubha built his church in the eighth century) we passed a sign that read, "Balnakeil Craft Village: Craft Workshops—Galleries—Visitors Welcome." I had read about the village and it sounded interesting, so we thought we would have a look. G had been a successful potter when I first met her at Oxford, and we are always interested in seeing work in progress. The village turned out to be more arresting as a social question than as a gallery experience and has left me confounded. How can creative craftsmen and women be content to live ugly?

A bit of background. In 1954 in the crofting township of Balnakeil in Sutherland County, just north of Durness and a few miles southeast of Cape Wrath, HM Armed Forces abandoned a partially completed collection of squat, flat-roofed concrete huts that were to have been an early warning radar station. To say this example of military architecture lacked character or sensitivity to the environment would be a gross understatement and generous in the extreme. In a word, it was ugly! The huts sat empty and deteriorated for nearly ten years. Then in 1963, a bright young development officer of the Sutherland County Council had an epiphany—the Far North Project. According to Ronald Lansley, one of the craftspeople, this was to be "a village where craftsmen and women in community drew upon the enchantment of their surroundings to create new formations, new ideas, new products." Clearly the enchanting surroundings lay outside the radar station.

The "village" was advertised throughout Britain, craftspeople applied, and those accepted were given very low rents of fifty pounds (seventy-five dollars) per year, plus considerable assistance to convert their radar station shells into habitable homes and working studios. After Balnakeil Craft Village was born in 1964, the Sutherland Council paid for advertising to get tourists to come, look, and buy. Although the cast changed from time to time, on average, fifteen craftspeople worked in the village at any given time—potter, painter, printmaker, weaver, enameller, ceramicist, sculptor, wood worker, leather worker, fly tier. Talent levels ranged from art to hobby. Personal goals spanned an equally broad range from laid back, mellow flower child to people like Ronald Lansley, who worked seriously at their crafts and were committed to the village concept.

Sculptor Lotte Glob is another example of the early "do it" group. Danish-born, she studied in Denmark, Ireland, and France and came to Balnakeil in her early twenties in 1968. She recently gave up on the village as a place to live, kept her studio there, and made a cottage in Laid on Loch Eriboll her home. Lotte is known for climbing mountains to beautiful isolated places where she "plants" one of her sculpted pots and records her experience—weather, time, what she feels, and what she sees. Lotte then photographs her pot in place, collects rocks and sediments from the area that will in time become part of a new sculpture, and heads on home. She has planted her sculptured pots all over the North West Highlands and calls these her "pot spots." Linked together, she says this is the "ultimate rock garden."

Over thirty-five years, some two hundred people have lived and worked in the Village. In 1980, after fifteen years of ownership and management, the Sutherland Council sold studio/homes to resident tenants at nominal prices. Fragile community bonds frayed even more since there was then no landlord to unite against. In 1983 some villagers tried to establish a cooperative improvement association. But between divergent values, wrangling, and indifference, the effort collapsed. Now, of the twenty households, around two-thirds remain craft-related, and a number of these are summer only. The population is aging. There are no pregnant women or preschool children, and sale prices of studios and homes are beyond what most young people can afford. There is not even the whiff of the original vision that "through their own commitment" craft workers would "create their own community to pursue their own enterprise in an unrivaled environment."

I asked several people why the "creative craft community" never took. The following are not literal quotes but are what the answers added up to.

- "Craft people by nature turn inward to create objects that are personal. 'Community' and 'artist' are contradictory terms."

- "You can't drop a new culture based on art into a dominant old culture based on crofting and expect the new culture to flower."

- "A bunch of the crafties were pot-smoking deadbeats along for the free ride."

- "Because they were craft people did not mean they had a common language or outlook and could communicate with each other on village matters."

- "What matters is not what a group of people have, but what they do. Look at the history of the clearances and crofters who worked their bad soil and with each other to build a pretty good life. Many of those who came to the village were self-absorbed kids who grew up in a welfare society and were used to taking without giving."

- "There was never any leadership."

Quite apart from the failure of community, what remains a conundrum for me is why have a group of people engaged in creative pursuits put so little effort into making their village and their homes more agreeable places to live? The village is a drab, depressing place. Many of the "huts" have unpainted, water-stained concrete walls or walls painted so long ago it makes no difference. Few flowers, shrubs, or trees have been planted to soften the harsh feeling. To all outward appearances, the people of Balnakeil Craft Village are content to live ugly.

Could it be that the ghosts of the abandoned early warning radar station still possess the soul of Balnakeil Craft Village?

A WELCOME CUPPA

WHEN WE LEFT PORT-NA-CON the morning of our visit to the craft village, the estimable Lesley suggested we might want to stop at the Loch Croispol Bookshop and Licensed Restaurant (LCBLR) for a "cuppa" and a chat with Simon Long, Anglican priest, chef, and co-owner. It turned out to be a very welcome suggestion because after the chill of the craft village we needed something to warm our hearts. Lesley hadn't told us she had arranged for Simon to give us a copy of Durness Past and Present, a community-produced booklet that has been a very useful resource.

The bookshop/restaurant is at the edge of the craft village. In sharp contrast to the village, it is a place of welcome and warmth. Eight tables are surrounded by floor-to-ceiling bookshelves holding an excellent collection of books on subjects ranging from Scottish history to poetry and music, and many books in Gaelic, "so that people can browse the bookshelves while eating and drinking." (The LCBLR logo is a salmon reading a book with the motto, "Food for Mind and Body.") Large windows along the west wall look out to the calm setting of Loch Croispol, with Balnakeil Bay beyond. A large children's section is arranged behind bookshelves at the south end of the dining area. With masses of children's books and beanbags to flop on, it makes for a great hideaway for kids and a quieter time at dinner for their parents.

LCBLR's boast of being the most northwesterly bookshop on the U.K. mainland is easy to verify because if you walk a little bit further on, you walk into the Atlantic. How this bookstore/restaurant got there is one more story of incomers finding fulfillment. As a young priest in the Church of England, Simon married an American woman and moved to the States in 1969. He served nineteen years in Episcopal dioceses in New Mexico, Kentucky, Nebraska, and South Dakota. (The Episcopal Church entered the colonies with settlers at Jamestown, Virginia, in 1607 as Church of England. The denomination became autonomous in 1789 as the Protestant Episcopal Church and has remained since then in communion with the Church of England.) In 1988, Simon, aged forty-seven and now divorced, came home to Britain and the diocese of Leicestershire, about a hundred miles north of London. Simon's bookstore/restaurant partner, Kevin Crowe, worked in social services for county government in nearby Suffolk.

Together, Simon and Kevin took a number of vacations in the North West Highlands. Like other incomers, they had become attached to west Sutherland's wild and peaceful beauty and the quality of life it offered. They also decided they were ready to add a new dimension to their lives. Well, as Simon told me, since his second calling was as a chef and Kevin was a lifelong bibliophile, what could be more logical than a bookstore/restaurant in Durness? And so they built one. At last report, bookstore, restaurant, Simon, and Kevin were doing fine.

OF GOD AND GOLF

ON A LOW HILL overlooking Balnakeil Bay next to the white sands of Balnakeil beach, with a view out to Feraid Head, is surely one of the more spectacular sites to be found for a church anywhere. All that remains now of the roofless Durness Old Church that had its first stones put in place in the twelfth century are ivy-clad front and back walls held together by a few feet of side wall and history reaching back to the seventh century.

St. Maelrubha, abbot and martyr (Danish Vikings did him in) with more than thirty churches and heaven only knows how many holy sites to his credit, was to church building in Scotland what the Stevensons were to lighthouses. St. Maelrubha, descended from Niall, King of Ireland, was born in 642 and in his thirtieth year sailed to Scotland from Ireland with a following of monks. After two years of traveling about, and founding his first six churches, he built his chief church and monastery in Applecross, a coastal village north of Skye "in the midst of pictish folk." He then set out on further missionary journeys and church building that in the late 600s or early 700s included the site now occupied by the Durness Old Church.

St. Maelrubha developed a strong reputation as an "interlocutor for heavenly favors." He was said to be "at the left ear of God" and was possessed of a talent for curing the insane. St. Maelrubha's well on the Isle Maree in Loch Maree played a significant role in the cure. The drill was to row the "patient of lunacy" to Isle Maree with a strong rope of horsehair tied firmly around the patient's waist and under both arms. Before docking, the boat circled the island three times clockwise, and on each lap the patient was dunked long and deep. After landing on the island, the water-logged patient first knelt before the altar as others prayed for the cure to take hold and was then plunged into St. Maelrubha's Well for a substantial drink of its curative waters. The treatment was topped off with an "offering" made by tying a ribbon to a holy oak tree next to the well and driving a coin edgeways into the trunk of the tree. Considering that this cure started in the ninth century and was still in practice more than a thousand years later (the last "cure" being reported in the Inverness Courier on 4 November 1857), it is just possible that St. Maelrubha did have something going with the heavenly father.

Recounting her visit to Isle Maree in 1877, Queen Victoria wrote of visiting St. Maelrubha's Well and following local tradition in a quest

Seabird high-rise on Handa Island

Razorbills on stage at Handa Island

Walk into the sea at Tarbet

Passing place on the single track to Tarbet

Turn right for Foindle

Foindle

Mother and triplets (one hiding) on a morning stroll at Loch Hope

Late afternoon on Loch Loyal

Stoer Head Lighthouse

A threatening day on Loch Eriboll with Ben Hope beyond

The end of a hard day's work

A session at The Ceilidh Place

John Gorman

Toad Patrol at Lochan Ordain

Warren Rovetch

Grades 5-7, Durness Primary School

Di Johnson (left) and Inge Ford, Little
Lodge proprietors

Lesley Black, Port-Na-Con Guest House
proprietor

Lesley Crosfield and Colin Craig, Albannach proprietors

for good luck. "We hammered some pennies into the tree, to the branches of which there are also rags and ribbons tied." The poet John Greenleaf Whittier celebrated the visit to the well with this offering:

> And whoso bathes therein his brow
> With care or madness burning,
> Feels once again his healthful thought
> And sense of peace returning.

With poetry like that, to quote Yogi Berra, "You gotta believe!"

While St. Maelrubha got close to God through good works, it is said of the Durness Old Church that a famous local villain, Donald MacMurdo, made a full faith effort to buy his way in.

According to *Durness Past and Present,* MacMurdo "raided all and everyone from his den on the east side of Loch Eriboll and was responsible for at least eighteen murders." When Uisdean Dubh MacKay, Second Lord of Reay was rebuilding the church in 1619, MacMurdo contributed 1,000 pounds (about $3 million in current dollars) on condition he be buried in a special vault in the church "to prevent my enemies from interfering with my remains." Money talks, and the inscription on MacMurdo's tomb, built into a niche in the south wall of the church, has a skull and crossbones and reads:

> Donald MacMurdo heir lyis lo
> Vasil to his friend, Var to his fo
> True to his maister in veird and vo
> DMMC   1623

Beside the tomb is a "hallowed stone." Immediately west of the church is the Durness Golf Club. The ninth hole requires a 155-yard drive into the wind across an inlet of the Atlantic. Local golf lore has it that rubbing the hallowed stone, and a short prayer including a request for divine guidance from St. Maelrubha, is sure to help with the ninth hole. I wonder if it also helps to quell "golf rage"? The magazine *Scottish Life* reports, "Despite having invented the sport of golf, Scottish golfers appear to be least equipped to deal with the game's frustrations." The article goes on to explain that thirty-one percent of Scottish golfers, versus twenty-five percent of golfers surveyed in England, experience "absolute frustration" with the game of golf. Even more worrisome is that "twice as many Scots are involved in violent confrontations on golf courses than golfers in the rest of Britain." Maybe the Pacific Highlands aren't as safe as we thought they were.

Course rules at Durness request golfers to "not disturb anglers when playing the 15th hole," which runs alongside Loch Lanish. The loch has a reputation for brown trout.

There is a problem no one has solved. A number of seabirds resident within range of an errant drive off the ninth tee keep trying to hatch golf balls.

BACK TO GO

IT HAS BEEN A wonderful journey—Inverness, North Erradale, Ullapool, Achiltibuie, Baddidarroch, Scourie, Port-Na-Con. And now, having been along on this journey of discovery, may I suggest you may find new meaning in Chapter 1, "Reflections," if you read it once again.

PART II

ON BEING
A TRAVELER

Last year I went around the world.
This year I think I'll go someplace else.

—TOURIST A TO TOURIST B

A TOURIST TASTES. A traveler savors. Independent travelers find rewards in both the journey and the destination. Your imagination dances. You leave the familiar behind while bringing much of yourself to the adventure. As Emerson wrote, "Though we travel the world over to find the beautiful, we must carry it with us or we find it not."

Creaky you may be, but you have the advantage of a large collection of experiences to draw on as you plan a satisfying and manageable journey. As your own travel planner you double your pleasure—daydreaming and anticipating (like a gardener planning next summer's blooms), and then experiencing the reality of your journey.

I will tell you a bit about how I went about planning our Highlands trip, offer a test for rating how "creaky" you are, and suggest a way you can create your own traveler's profile. There is also a list of essentials for travelers.

How Florence Led to the Highlands

WHEN G AND I started thinking about the Highlands trip, we reflected on our trip the year before. First was a short stop in London to see
friends from our Oxford days—when G was a studio potter and I was
a Fulbright scholar in the early 1950s. We found London dirtier, hard-
er to get around in, more ethnically diverse, and as exciting as ever.
Then it was on to Italy. We started at Bellagio on Lake Como with a fair
amount of lazing about on a veranda, looking through a mass of spring
flowers at the blue lake and gliding from one town to another on lake
steamers. We had a lovely corner room at the Hotel Metropole with a
tiny balcony and a view up, down, and across the lake, because I had
faxed the hotel a photo from their brochure with a circle round the
windows of the room we wanted, and had it confirmed.

Next, we drove the Superstrada (which Italians treat as a competitive sport) to Lucca, a walled Tuscan city we couldn't get into
for hours because we arrived on eco-day, when no cars were
allowed. After an hour of pleading, G remembered she had our
automobile card with the universal icon for handicapped drivers in
her purse. The gates opened and minutes later we were at the
Piccolo Hotel Puccini looking out the window of another corner
room, this time to the Piazza Puccini, with a statue of Giacomo
Puccini smack in the center.

Every time I looked out the window, there was another weary tour
group pausing for a sixty-second look and lecture before being led on
by their intrepid leader. Other Lucca images remain. One was the elegant policewoman astride her fine white horse, holding a cell phone
to her ear with one hand and gesticulating forcefully with the other,
with the horse quite happily taking care of itself. Another—a father
pedaling away, one hand steering his rickety bike, the other with a
cell phone to his ear, an infant on the crossbar in front of him, tod-
dler in a seat behind, and everyone happy. Our next stop was
Castellina in Chianti, where we spent a few quiet days in vineyards,
enjoyed a brilliant view from our exorbitantly large room across a

valley to Tuscan hills beyond, and found any number of pleasant hill towns to visit (including one that specialized in grappa).

And then Florence. In retrospect, I think we went to Florence out of a sense of obligation. In a half a dozen trips to Italy, we had never been to Florence. After all, everyone goes to Florence and raves about it. The first omen of problems ahead was not being able to find our hotel and being trapped in high-exhaust, high-speed traffic with daredevil motorcyclists darting in and out. There was no correlation between our street map and street signs. Finally, in desperation, I hired a taxi to lead me to our hotel, wait while we checked in, lead me to Hertz, and take me back to the hotel.

I had chosen this perfect "small hotel with a helpful staff" on the Via Cavour after careful research. The Guelfo Bianco was located about a block from the Duomo and within easy walking range of other premium Florence sights. Our room at the back of the hotel was comfortable and quiet with good views over the ocher-colored roofs of Florence. After a recovery rest, we decided to undertake a quiet exploration of the neighborhood. One step out the front door and—wham—into a wall of Florentine noise that never seemed to stop. It wasn't just good old common noise. Imagine a very high level of traffic noise punctuated every few seconds by the high-pitched whine of a gaggle of snowmobiles combined with the *grrrum, grrrum* and roar of a gang of guys on Harley Hogs. Another two steps down the Via Cavour, and right next to us a black Mercedes hit a bicycle in the street. The kid flew off and landed at G's feet. Fortunately, he only broke an arm.

Well, the best of plans can go awry. Lesson number one: when things start to go bad, check out and move someplace else, or leave town. We should have headed for the hills. You will probably have a wonderful time in Florence, as so many people do.

Planning Our Highlands Trip

Thinking About Where to Go. With Florence in our mind, the quiet, the relative isolation, rugged beauty, and easy, short drives from place to place of the North West Highlands had great appeal. G and I had been to the Island of Mull in the Hebrides off the West Highlands coast and loved it. Friends had recently been to the Atlantic Highlands and had glowing things to say. So we moved from the "maybe" to the "messing around" phase. I looked at a few standard guidebooks, ordered up whatever the Highlands of Scotland Tourist Board had to offer, and began exploring the Web. The richest veins were sites produced by local authorities about their areas and sites on which professional photographers displayed their wares. The best sites are listed in Appendix I. I also made sure I was on the lowest-cost direct dial international phone program. Ten cents a minute makes it easy to get answers by phone.

Decision and Tickets. In the end several things helped us decide on the North West Highlands of Scotland: good flights—nonstop on British Airways from Denver to Gatwick, with connections to Inverness; the number of appealing small guest houses in good spots to choose from; photos showing the haunting beauty of the Atlantic seaboard; the revival of Gaelic music; seeing Suilven; and back roads to interesting and isolated places. We decided in November to go the next May, since May and September are the best months for the Highlands. We locked in our travel dates and bought paper tickets with senior discounts. If ticket prices go up before you depart, you have been smart to buy your tickets early. If prices go down, most airlines will give you a credit for the difference, which you can apply on another ticket. So after buying tickets, it's worth checking back from time to time. Getting tickets early also gives you a better choice of seats. I always choose paper tickets because they are evidence for security clearance; they make it easier to change flights if there are delays, cancellation, or missed flights; and they work even when computer systems go down.

Choosing a Rental Car. While prices charged by different airlines on the same routes are usually comparable, there tends to be a wide variation in rental rates for cars in the same class. Classes are subcompact (sardine cans), compact, intermediate, and on up. I have done subcompact and compact and been sorry because of road noise, discomfort, and a feeling of vulnerability on highways. I now go for intermediate. Beyond that, my concerns include price, model, and the number and location of rental stations in the area we will travel (in case the car has problems and I need to exchange it). As to model, I want to be able to get in and out of the car without bumping my head, sit up high with good road vision, have an engine with enough power to climb steep hills, get a color we can live with for a month, and have a tape deck for music of our choice along the way. We can't get all this all the time, but we can try.

I called the Hertz, Avis, and Budget agents in Inverness and asked which model they would choose if they were over seventy and driving single track roads. We ended up with a five-speed Ford Focus from Hertz. With "petrol" at six dollars a gallon and cars with automatic transmissions consuming twenty-five percent more of it, the gas-saving manual shift was fine with me. The monthly price quoted by Hertz was the best, the station manager in Scotland sounded like she knew what she was talking about, and I tried out the Focus at a Boulder dealer and liked it. Prices tend to be lower if you rent far ahead. I followed my usual practice of checking back on rental prices every month or six weeks, since you can hit a special promotion or a rate change. (It worked for me this time.) Airline mileage club, AAA, AARP, and other discounts apply. Rental agents will tell you which of these offers the best discount. I also found that, at least for this trip, Internet rates were not as good as those live people offered.

The Cell Phone Question. After reading about the "wee mad road," the "Breakdown Zone," and isolated spots where you might not see another car, much less another soul, for days on end, I decided to rent a cell phone for emergency use. Because of different systems, most

U.S. cell phones will not work in Europe. So I rented a phone for forty-five dollars for the month, plus air time charges. It arrived as promised via FedEx in a nice, neat carry case that fit well in my suitcase, and I was able to give everyone our global telephone number. With this build-up, as you may have guessed, I had zero airtime on the phone. I called no one and no one called me. The wee mad road was a challenge, but not disabling. Perhaps having a phone for emergencies is like carrying around an umbrella so it won't rain. Whether or not you have a cell phone, do make sure you have an MCI, AT&T, or other calling card plan that permits you to direct dial calls to the U.S. at relatively low cost. These plans are cheaper than cell phone time charges and most certainly cheaper than hotel long distance rates.

Deciding Where to Stay. We are always looking for more than a bed because where we stay is an essential part of the whole travel experience. What we looked for on this trip was an amalgam of things that would make the guest houses we chose very special—distinctive character, personality of the proprietor, reputation for a good kitchen, view from the dining room and bedroom (seeing Suilven out the window), location in relation to things we wanted to see and do, number of rooms (we wanted to stay in small places), and, of course, price. So choosing where we stay became a big part of our planning effort. Our scorecard on this trip was pretty good. Three places were better than expected, one was a little worse than expected, and two were on target.

First I assembled my working tools. I started with the *Ordnance Survey: Northern Scotland* at a scale of one inch to four miles. Later, when we knew the territory we were going to cover more clearly, I got maps at one-and-a-quarter inch to one mile that show detail down to lighthouses and picnic tables. From the Highlands of Scotland Tourist Board I got publications covering bed-and-breakfasts, guest houses, and hotels that included "quality assured ratings," details on the number of rooms with and without bathrooms, special features like fishing and pony trekking, prices, some photographs, and brief statements by owners as to why you would want to stay with them. I added to these a couple of commercial guidebooks that offered frank opinions on places to stay. While web sites offered a good bit about the areas, they didn't add much to the other material, and, anyway, it's hard to take my computer to bed.

With working tools in hand, it was back and forth between the most scenic, least traveled areas, a preliminary itinerary, and lists of four or five of the most desirable-sounding places to stay at each stop. I then faxed a letter to each potential choice asking about availability for specific dates and rates—which can vary up and down from published rates—and requested a brochure plus material about their area. I find it useful to read what people say about their places and how they present themselves. Based on what I received, I made preliminary choices and then phoned the proprietor at each place with questions about the weather at the time of year we would be there, what the rooms were like, if the rooms got a lot of natural daylight (very important to G), and so on. If a proprietor doesn't sound particularly warm and welcoming, or something else is out of whack, I move on to the next choice. By the time a reservation was made we had not only chosen the place we would stay and frequently the room we would have, but we also had some idea of the personality of the proprietor. We agree with Sherlock Holmes who says in *A Case of Identity*, "It has been an axiom of mine that the little things are infinitely the most important."

Daydreaming. Having dealt with the essentials, I then settled down to serious daydreaming; finding out more about the territory we would travel; looking for teahouses, restaurants, and pubs worth considering; and absorbing a bit of history and what is happening in England and Scotland. The best web site for news is the British Broadcasting Company (news.bbc.co.uk), where I was able to go to news on Scotland. *The Times of London* (www.thetimes.co.uk) and the *Guardian* (www.guardian.co.uk) are well-known newspapers with sites. The site for the most northern mainland newspaper is appropriately named The Northern Times (www.northern-times.co.uk).

Trip Journal. I find a trip journal an essential tool. Mine, kept in a spiral notebook, included all essential travel details—reservation locator number (the code airlines use to track reservations), flight numbers, seat numbers, departure and arrival times, and airline telephone numbers in the U.S. and overseas. I noted the same range of information for the car rental and took the reservation confirmation that included dates, requested car model, and rates that I had Hertz fax to me. Then I had a separate page for each place we would stop that included dates, address, proprietor name(s), telephone, fax number, e-mail address, and what we might want to see or do in the area (waterfall, lighthouse, pub with Gaelic music sessions, special view, and so on). Toad crossings and perfect walks fall under the "happenings" category and are the type of information you are not likely to discover by any amount of advance research. Essential correspondence, reservation confirmations, and "take with" material were in a few separate files.

How Creaky Are You? A Test

AT THE END OF a trip you should not have to come home to recover. You may reach a limit on your capacity to absorb new experiences, but you should not arrive home creakier and more tired than when you left. When planning your journey and your destinations, be realistic on just how creaky you are. Here are some questions to ask yourself and blanks for you to enter your ratings on a 1 to 5 scale. 1 is best and equals not much or easy and 5 is worst and equals lots or hard.

Creaky Test	Rate 1-5

1. How long can I be on my feet and walking around until I really need to sit down? 90 minutes = 1; 15 minutes = 5 _____
2. How many city blocks can I walk at a time?
   1 block = 5; 5 blocks = 1
   • With a cane _____
   • Without a cane _____

3. Can I tie my shoes bending over with my feet
   on the floor or do I have to rest each foot on
   a curb or a chair to tie my shoe? (If you wear only
   slip-ons to avoid tying laces, it's a 5.)   _____
4. Do I feel dizzy when I bend over or get up quickly?   _____
5. When I climb or descend stairs, do I need
   to use a handrail?   _____
6. How easy or hard is it for me to walk up/down
   a slope or small hill?   _____
7. Can I lift a suitcase into the airplane luggage
   bin and get it down?   _____
8. Can I put my pants (or skirt) on while standing up
   without having to hold on to something for support?   _____
9. Do my joints and/or my back ache? Never?
   Sometimes? Always?   _____

TOTAL _____

If you scored 40 or more, get back in bed. Otherwise, start planning
your trip.

A Few Essentials

Here are a few basics every Creaky Traveler should remember:

- Take a miracle spot remover with you.

- Nikes or Reeboks are a tourist giveaway. If you really want to
  make sure locals can spot you, add a water bottle, baseball cap,
  and sunglasses.

- Almost everything will cost more than you had expected.

- Leave time each day for the unexpected.

- If you don't have a cane, get one. It will help you walk and encourage other people to be considerate of your needs. Folding canes are easy to put into a tote bag.

- Always request a wheelchair to and from planes. Make this request at the time you make your reservation, repeat it at check-in, and mention it again to a steward or stewardess on the flight. You do not have to be disabled for a wheelchair, only needful. Airport walking distances can be incredibly long, particularly at the end of an international flight when going to customs and baggage check.

- Choose an airplane seat that meets your needs—an aisle seat if you drink as much water as you should and use the lavatory more often than younger folk.

- Always check to make sure your hotel room is on a floor you can manage if there isn't an elevator. Remember, in Europe the floor count starts with ground floor and then one, two, three, et cetera. So in American terms the European third floor is the American fourth.

- If you read in bed, the first thing to do when you get to your room is to check to see if there is a bedside lamp and if the light bulb wattage is adequate. If there is no lamp, ask for one. If the bulb has low wattage, ask for a better one. When making your reservation, mention you are a bed reader (but more often than not, this is forgotten).

- Walking somewhere may be easy, but getting back can be a trial. Plan ahead. For museums, find out if there is a coffee shop where you can take a break. In Venice, I always chose restaurants for dinner that were near a Vaporetto (water bus) stop. Strolling to dinner was always lovely, but after dinner we wanted an easy way home.

- Take it really slow the first few days after moving through five or more time zones. There are a zillion "how to help your body make the change" plans. The essential part of any of them is to ease into your trip. It is especially important not to do much the first day. I am also a believer in sleeping pills to help get at least a few hours sleep on the brief overnight flight to Europe, and to get to sleep the first few nights (when 11:00 P.M. is still 4:00 P.M. for your body). Check with your doctor. There are brands that don't leave a hangover.

- Asolare, an Italian term that means doing next to nothing and enjoying it, is an essential rule of travel—an afternoon with a book in a café or lolling by a stream tossing sticks in the water to see where they drift.

- When you return, don't try to sneak any prohibited items back in. These include products made from sea turtles; ivory; fur of spotted cats; wild bird feathers; crocodile leather; chunks of coral; and fresh fruit, vegetables, or meat.

- Most of all ask, ask, ask and tell, tell, tell. Let people know of any special needs you have. Airlines in particular say their greatest problem is people reticent about telling them of special needs in advance because they don't want to make a fuss. I am always astounded at the number of people who won't ask to have their table changed in a restaurant if they have been given a terrible one. Declan Halpin, the excellent British Airways station manager in Denver, told me about older and other people collapsing on the long walk from their planes to customs simply because they didn't want to be a bother and ask for a wheel chair—and about how much easier it is for an airline to provide a wheelchair than emergency medical services.

TRAVELER'S SELF-PROFILE

THE PLACES YOU WANT to put on your "hope to go to" travel list; the kinds of guest houses, hotels, or bed-and-breakfasts you want to stay in; the types of things you want to see and do; the types of experiences that will indulge your senses—these are among the questions you can begin to answer in your traveler's self-profile. The essence of a self-profile is to accept the axiom "different strokes for different folks."

For example, when planning my trip to the Highlands, had I been a devoted fly fisherman, my daydreams would have put me in the shallows of Loch Loyal landing the biggest brown trout ever, and that evening at dinner, having the size of this prize catch announced to the other envious fishermen staying at the inn. Or if I were a hill walker or climber, I would see myself surveying my kingdom from the top of Suilven. As it was, G and I were doing exactly what we had daydreamed about—quietly and casually inhaling the raw and penetrating natural beauty of the Atlantic Highlands as we meandered about, listening to lots of Gaelic music, staying at small, comfortable, distinctive guest houses, and leaving enough time for lovely and unexpected things to happen to us. If museums, symphony concerts, swish hotels, and the club scene had been our thing, we would have been in Edinburgh, Glasgow, or London.

So begin your personal traveler's profile now and change it and add to it as you travel more. If you travel with a partner, the merging of interests and profiles becomes more complicated. You have a choice: think on it together, or one thinks for two. Profile questions I would ask myself are listed below. As you go along, add and answer your own questions. For some of the questions, before you answer, sit back, close your eyes, and picture yourself acting out your answer. If a warm glow comes on, you are in business. Also, as you go along keep notes, and when done write your profile as if you were describing your traveler self to someone else.

1. What was the best trip I ever took? What made it so good? What particular experiences on the "best trip" are especially memorable? On other trips? (Think of the things you tell other people when recalling a trip.) What experiences do I remember because they were bad?

2. Am I afflicted with "traveler's remorse," anxiety from having missed something on my "must see or do" list? If I am somewhere I really like, am I willing to stay with it and skip something else?

3. What are my physical limitations—driving, walking, climbing? How easily do I tire? If I overexert, am I out of action the next day? What time do I usually go to bed? Get up? How deeply am I committed to this schedule?

4. What areas of interest turn me on—art, history, geology, geography, botany/gardens, archeology, cultural anthropology, opera, wildlife, traditional music?

5. Given the choice, would I prefer an evening in a pub, eating pub food (much of it frozen and deep-fried these days) and talking with locals, or would I prefer having an excellent five-course dinner at a superior restaurant? Or would I choose both?

6. Do I prefer crowded days with every minute planned out, or am I comfortable leaving things open? Do I wait to see how I feel in the morning before deciding how to start that day, or do I forge ahead no matter what? What if it's raining hard?

7. Do I need social interaction? Do I like to share experiences and ideas with other people? Do I prefer to stay at a guesthouse or a small hotel where guests mingle? Have breakfast and dinner together? Am I a good party person? Or am I at the other end of the string and happy to keep my own company? Or some of both?

8. How do I respond to physical environment? Does it make a real difference to me if my bedroom has good natural light and is well and cleanly furnished versus being a little dark and on the dingy side? View or no view? Do I insist on having a bathroom with my room, or is one down the hall okay? Am I willing to spend time to search out somewhere special to stay, or am I more concerned with what I do during the day than where I lay my head at night?

9. How do I indulge my senses? With a walk in a field of wildflowers or losing my way in a maze of back streets in an ancient city? Or either, at different times, in different places? What really gets to me, deeply? Memorably?

10. Do I crave adventure? Or does safety come first? Do I easily feel threatened?

11. How much time can I devote to travel that takes me far from home? Is this once a year or more often?

12. How much can I afford to spend? Would I choose going for a longer time and staying in less-expensive places? Rent a smaller car to save money? Eat less expensive meals? Or would I choose to live it up a bit for a shorter time?

Now, review your notes and write them up, and you will have your personal traveler's profile. Read it over the next time you start thinking about a trip.

Some of Everything You Ever Wanted to Know

Since I don't know what you already know, here is a lot of what I know. Take your pick.

BEFORE YOUR TRIP

Home. These are largely matters of security. (1) Complete post office form #8076, "Authorization to Hold Mail," telling the post office to hold your mail beginning on a specific date. (2) Schedule stop and restart of newspaper delivery. (3) If you will be away during the growing season, have someone cut your lawn and water your flowers to keep up appearances. (4) Set up an automatic on/off system for lights and radio. (5) Let neighbors and police know you will be away, and if someone will be house sitting or stopping by to check your house periodically. (6) The day you leave, unplug all small appliances and set the thermostat at fifty-five to sixty degrees. (7) Give a house key to a friend or neighbor for emergencies, which could include you losing your key.

Documents and Records. (1) If you don't have a passport, apply for one. If you have one, check the expiration date. Issuance of a new passport can take up to twelve weeks (but ordinarily takes less time). You can do it through most post offices. (2) Make sure your credit cards won't expire while you are on your trip. Credit card companies will advance renewal dates if needed. (3) Photocopy your passport cover page, driver's license, and credit cards in case of loss or theft. Make a note of credit card company phone number(s) in case of card loss, your flight schedule, flight numbers, itinerary, and related phone numbers along the way. Give a copy of all this to a friend/relative and take a copy with you.

Credit Cards, Currency, and Insurance. (1) Make sure you know your credit card and debit card Personal Identification Number (PIN) for ATM use. Also, if you don't have a debit card, get one, since debit cards make more sense than credit cards for ATM cash withdrawals. If you use a credit card for ATM cash, high interest rate charges begin from the date of withdrawal. With debit cards you pay only a transaction fee. The best plan is to get a hundred dollars or so in the currency of the country that will be your first stop and then use ATM machines when you get there. Never use hotels or exchange bureaus. They always have poorer exchange rates. Credit cards are fine to use for hotel bills, restaurants, and other purchases. These charges show up in the normal way on your next bill. Keep receipts and always check for overcharges. Also, before traveling, check on credit card transaction fees for conversion of foreign currency charges to dollars. These charges ordinarily run around two percent, but can vary by card. The reason using credit and debit cards makes sense is that your charges are bundled with those of thousands of other people and converted to dollars at the wholesale million dollar rate. In the simplest terms, credit card companies can buy dollars cheaper than you can. (2) Most domestic auto insurance does not extend to overseas rentals. Many credit cards will include coverage on foreign rentals. This means you don't have to buy all of the expensive added coverage offered. Several cautions are in order. Some cards exclude coverage in certain countries. For example, American Express won't provide insurance coverage for cars rented in Italy. Some MasterCards restrict coverage to a maximum number of rental days. Other cards provide damage coverage but not theft. Ask for printed copies of restrictions and then use the card that works best for you, whether you prepay before you leave or pay when you return the car. (3) Some cards include "global assist," which can include medical evacuation and other overseas services. Check it all out.

Health. (1) If you have a medical condition or are on long-term medication, check with your doctor to see if any precautions are in order while flying or traveling. Advise the airline when making your reservation if there is anything they need to know about your condition that might require oxygen in flight—for example, asthma or emphysema. (2) Check with your doctor about medication, including, if you think you need either, sleeping pills and anti-inflammatory pills. Also, get a prescription or note saying you need your cane with you for "medical" reasons, just in case airport security classifies canes as a weapon. I checked with airport security in advance and was told we would need cane "prescriptions." We got them and then weren't asked for them once. But you never know. (3) Get copies of all prescriptions by generic name to take with you in case you lose your medication and need prescriptions refilled overseas. In some countries the simplest thing to do may be to have a new supply shipped to you in one or two days via UPS or FedEx—Great Britain, yes; Italy, no. (4) Keep medication in the original containers pharmacists supply—a caution because of concerns over illegal drugs. (5) If you wear glasses or contacts, make sure you have an extra pair/set.

Travel Insurance. There are companies that issue single travel policies that cover nearly everything—trip cancellation, lost or late luggage, travel accidents, travel medical, and medical evacuation. And then there are policies for any one of these items. Opting for travel insurance is a personal thing. I don't ordinarily get coverage, and others would never think of going without it. Many Medigap and other health insurance policies will pay for overseas medical costs. Just keep your receipts. Also, in Great Britain and some other countries with national health services, emergency services will be provided without charge.

Security and Money. This is really a question of where you will be traveling. In the Atlantic Highlands you could pin money on your sleeve and other than being thought a bit eccentric, you and your money would be completely safe. In Naples, it's another matter. Many people are comfortable with a money belt or a "neck safe." With ATMs nearly everywhere there is no need to carry a lot of money with you at any time. Traveler's checks are almost a thing of the past. The items needing protection are your passport, which you don't need to carry with you at all times, and credit cards that you probably will have all the time. I once had a pair of "travel trousers" with hidden pockets and zipper pockets, but they were more trouble than they were worth. There are a few basic rules to follow. For men, keep your wallet thin and carry it in a side pocket, never in your hip pocket. I keep a small, thin "wallet" for credit cards and my driver's license in one side pocket, and my cash in a money clip in the other side pocket. For women, don't carry any handbags hanging at your hip that a thief can grab, and don't wear any gold neck chains. If someone spills mustard on you, apologizes, and starts to help clean it off, forget it. It's an old pickpocket ploy. He helps you, an accomplice picks you, and the third member of the team stands by for the hand-off. So, be wary but not paranoid in airports and other crowded places. And never hang a camera or a handbag over the back of a chair in a café.

Toting Books. All books get heavier and heavier as a trip goes on. If there is travel information I want to take along that goes beyond what I have noted in my trip journal, I will copy the few pages that interest me. If it is a whole chapter, I will tear it out of the book and staple it together. Book lovers may see this as uncaring. Travelers see it as a necessity. As to general reading, G and I will agree on two paperbacks each and trade when we finish. We tend to read less than we think we will because there is so much else to do. Also, many guesthouses and bed-and-breakfasts have large collections of paperbacks left by previous guests and are happy to have you trade a book of yours for one in their collection.

PACKING

No matter what I say you will take too much. I take too much, G takes too much. Try as we might, even using carry-on size cases for a month of travel, we come home saying the same thing. We took too much. For what it's worth, here is advice from a packer with a qualified track record.

- Travel with a maximum of one roll-aboard (carry-on with wheels), even if you plan to check it, plus one carry-on tote bag. My tote bag is a small backpack with wheels. G's is a small tote that she can hook onto her suitcase. All roll-aboards should have a hook or other means of attaching the tote bag. There will be times when you are on your own and have to get your case from here to there—curb to check-in counter, car to guesthouse. Stay away from expensive suitcases. They identify you as a worthy target for thieves, and you are pained if the expensive suitcase gets damaged. I have a case with a lifetime guarantee I bought ten years ago. The guarantee actually worked when the handle broke last year. I could replace the case today for under seventy dollars. I think G paid thirty-nine dollars for her case many years ago. Be sure to tie colorful yarn or another easy-to-recognize identifier on your suitcase handle. Many suitcases look alike, and your personal identifier will help you spot your bag coming at you on the baggage return and keep someone else from mistaking yours for theirs. For "just in case," put your name, home address, and the address and telephone number of where you will be the first night inside your suitcase.

- In the tote bag, pack all your medication and eye stuff; reading material (you may not like what the plane has); a sweater in case the plane gets too cool at night; a small, refillable water bottle (some airlines distribute bottled water, others don't); moisturizer, because airplane air dries you out; and, if you plan to check your bag and are a worrier, a change of underwear and socks in case your checked bag is delayed or lost.

- These are the guidelines for what to take. (1) Clothes—layers for climate variation, colors that don't show dirt and are also coordinated for mix and match, wash-and-wear material that dries reasonably quickly. In Great Britain, a wash-and-wear oxford cloth shirt is unlikely to dry overnight, while a broadcloth shirt has a reasonable chance of doing so. The safety-first washing rules are to do your washing the first night of a two-night stay in case extra drying time is needed, and take extra plastic bags for packing wet clothes. Europeans believe Americans are obsessive about cleanliness, and we probably are. But as a traveler, try wearing clothes a little longer than you would at home. Also, most of the world has gone casual, not sloppy, like wearing sweaters where only a jacket used to do. Take posh only if you plan to stay posh where, for example, the correct thing is to dress for dinner. Even then, for men posh can mean a sport jacket but no tie. (2) Comfortable walking shoes. (3) Creams and liquids—put all of them in plastic containers, and pack the containers in plastic bags for double protection against spills. (4) Basic kit—compact umbrella, travel alarm, sewing kit, spot remover, small flashlight, washcloth in a plastic bag (many places don't provide washcloths), sunscreen (for the hopeful), vitamins, soap, small packages of Kleenex, and a first-aid kit with band aids, antiseptic cream, aspirin, diarrhea tablets, and a few prunes. (5) Plastic bag for dirty clothes. (6) A raincoat or rain jacket—pack one or carry one.

- And then there is the old how-to-pack argument between the "folders" and the "rollers." Take your choice. Rollers argue that when you roll up shirts, jeans, et cetera, you get more in and no creasing. Folders argue that with reasonable care and underwear or plastic bags in folds, everything comes out neat. Also, folded clothes make it easier to see what you have and to live out of your suitcase. Whether you roll or fold or some of both, remember there is room in your shoes and corners. Arrange clothes so your case is full and things won't jumble when baggage handlers start throwing your case around. G and I are folders and we unpack as little as possible. When we check in we ask for suitcase stands or put our cases on top of chests of drawers. One very important reminder is to pack no later than the day before you leave home on a trip, or else at the last minute you will start throwing things in for fear of forgetting something.

GETTING THERE AND BACK WELL AND SANE

I read *John Adams* by David McCullough and marveled at Adams' month-long crossing of the Atlantic in a sailing ship in the late 1700s as he went to take up a European post. What a sense of time and distance thirty days at sea must have offered. I was reminded of my own journeys to England between 1946 and the early 1950s on the SS Brazil, the Mauretania, and the Queen Mary, trips that lasted from eight to fourteen days. You knew you were going somewhere, and your mind and body were able to make an accommodating transition during these days at sea. Today, you and two hundred or three hundred other closely packed souls hurtle through the air and land jet-lagged at an airport that is different only in some small degree from the one you left eight hours or so before. No wonder you need to take pains to make this part of your travel experience manageable—especially if, like most people, you are traveling coach. So here are a few considerations and suggestions.

Choosing Airlines, Flights, and Seats

The serious traveler—creaky and other—looks for a balance between cost, airline, schedule, and seating.

Schedule. There are daytime flights to Europe from several East Coast cities. If you can manage any of these flights, great. The flight is seven hours, with a five-hour change in time. You leave around 9:00 A.M., get in around 9:00 P.M., have a light bite, stroll around a bit, and go off to bed. Your flight is more likely to be an overnight one. Suggestions: (1) Maximize air time/sleep time. If you leave for Europe from an East Coast airport, you have no choice. With a flight of seven hours, between dinner and breakfast you will be lucky to have three hours for a nap. If you fly nonstop from the West Coast, you have ten to eleven hours in the air, allowing a reasonable amount of time for sleep. So the trick is to choose a flight or get routed for maximum sleep time. For example, from Denver to London or Frankfurt you have choices—a United Airlines flight with a plane change in Chicago or Washington, or a nonstop flight on British Airways or

Lufthansa, with about nine hours in the air. (2) Leave late. If you fly into London, Paris, or anywhere else in the early morning and are staying in the city that day, you may well have a problem getting into your hotel room until hours later. I can remember once sitting around in the lobby of the Basil Street Hotel in London for five hours with my wife and daughters, waiting for a room. So leaving for your ocean hop as late as possible in the evening and getting in later in the morning is a good idea.

Seats. Coach seats are no joy in the best of situations, so try to make the best of one with the right seat on the right plane. (1) Improve your odds. Different airlines configure seats on the same type of aircraft in different ways. For example, on Boeing 777s both United Airlines and British Airways seat nine across. United Airlines seats two-five-two, or two seats at one window, five in the middle and two at the other window. British Airways does three-three–three. Lufthansa flies the Airbus 340 from Denver to Frankfurt with two-four-two seating. Sitting on the aisle of a two-seat row is my choice. G goes for the window. Two suggestions. Buy your ticket earlier for the best choice of seats. Find out which day of the week the flight you want has the lightest load, because even with three across the middle seat could be empty. (2) Should you choose an aisle or window seat? If you want the freedom to get up and move around the plane or go to the john any time, without disturbing anyone, go for an aisle seat. But remember, other people have to crawl over you or you have to get up to let them out. At the window you have the pleasure of a view and no one crawls over you, but you have to ask someone to move whenever you want get up. One other advantage of a window seat is that when the flight attendant asks for shades down to convert the airplane into a movie theatre, you don't have to. But, if you can't bear to disturb other people, do not sit at the window. (3) Some airlines place wheelchair passengers further forward. If you do use a wheelchair, ask.

FLYING HEALTHY

HERE IS WHERE YOU have to take control to survive the assault of flying on mind and body. You face three problems. First, the airplane is not a healthy environment. It is at best surface clean, and at least a few passengers will be passing around the odd germ. Second, even if the correct proportion of fresh air is brought in and circulated versus stale air is being recirculated (which uses less fuel), air is still dry and a cause of dehydration. Your third problem is "circadian dyschronism," more commonly known as jet leg. Somehow most of us survive all these problems and go on to have a good time. Here are a few suggestions to help boost your odds for flying healthy.

Before Your Flight. (1) Get a good night's sleep to ready for the battle. (2) Make sure your tote bag has everything you need in it—all your medication, moisturizer, antibacterial wipes, eye shade, ear plugs, water bottle, a sweater if the plane gets chilly, and reading material or puzzles to help your mind move toward sleep. Some airlines like British Airways provide coach passengers with kits containing an eyeshade, booties, toothbrush, and toothpaste. Others like United Airlines do not provide kits, so check beforehand. (3) Eat lightly the evening before and day of your flight. (4) Wear loose-fitting, comfortable clothing. (5) Get to the airport early and don't carry any heavy bags.

For Your Flight. When you check in, make sure any special requests have been noted in your computer record—wheelchair at all take off and arrival points, special meals if you have ordered them, and the seats that had been reserved for you. Seat assignments have a strange way of changing on occasion. On the flight follow these healthy flying rules:

- Figure out how your seat and footrest work. As a technology-deprived person, I find seat mechanics a challenge. Make sure you can keep your legs elevated, because even a little is important to circulation. Make sure you have a pillow and a blanket.

- Take your shoes off, or at a minimum, loosen the laces. For a fact, your feet will swell during the flight because of low air pressure and high altitude. Give your feet lots of room!

- Drink moderate amounts of alcohol or drinks with caffeine, or better yet, none at all. Do drink lots of water. The recommended dosage is one eight-ounce glass for every hour of flight. This is to compensate for dehydration caused by dry air.

- Do simple exercises in your seat, tensing each muscle in turn and holding for five seconds—shoulder, back, arms, legs, ankles, and buttocks—and move your feet a lot. Don't cross your legs for long or keep your hands clasped behind your head. Both limit circulation. More important, get out of your seat and walk up and down the aisle. You get to look at the amazing array of passengers, get a little exercise, and most importantly, move your blood around to limit any chance of deep vein thrombosis (DVT), sometimes called "economy class syndrome."

- Women, don't wear makeup other than lipstick, because makeup will help dry out your skin. Do use moisturizer during and at the end of the flight. Men, you too.

- When the feeling hits you, don't hesitate to nap. More importantly, sleep at least a few hours in the night. If your doctor approves, use sleeping pills. Some people swear by melatonin, which you can buy without a prescription. But you should still check with your doctor before using melatonin because of potential interaction with medication you may be taking.

- If you have requested a wheelchair at the end of the flight, mention this to cabin staff. They will make sure it is at the plane door for you. If you have an hour or more for connections, most airlines have what they call a "serenity room" for wheelchair passengers.

You can be dropped off and picked up again before your flight. Don't hesitate to use it. Try to remember, the airlines are happy for you not to become a problem.

- When landing, to keep your ears from blocking, use the diver's nose hold. Hold your nose and blow. This works best if you do it every five minutes or so starting about half an hour before landing.

After Your Flight. I am always surprised at the number of people who come home sick after traveling. It is usually a cold or some stomach complaint. These people have not listened to their bodies. Problems begin with trying to ignore jet lag—decreased concentration, irritability, and aching joints. The excitement and adrenaline rush that comes at the start of a stay in a new place can blur the problem but not eliminate it. Many businesses and government agencies have rules against their people doing any business the first day after a trip that involves three or more hours of time change.

For the sake of your whole journey, ease into the beginning. Some younger folks manage to get off the plane and through the day, eating and sleeping on the local time. If G and I are staying in the city where we have landed, we try to nap for an hour or so before setting out. Then we take a stroll for mild exercise and exposure to daylight to give our circadian rhythm a signal to start adjusting to a new reality. At bedtime try a warm shower, sleeping pill (we know someone who uses Nyquil), and an unexciting read, and you will be gone. With luck, the next thing you will hear is a call to breakfast.

Move into high gear over the span of a couple of days (although G and I seldom ever get there), and never, never drive very far the first day you have landed.

Bon voyage, travelers!

PLACES, SITES, AND SOURCES

PLACES WE STAYED

Diarmid Troup
Felstead Guest House
18 Ness Bank
Inverness IV2 4SF, Scotland
Phone/Fax: 44-1463-231-634
E-mail: felsteadgh@aol.com

Di Johnson and Inge Ford
Little Lodge
North Erradale
Gairloch, Wester Ross IV21 2D, Scotland
Phone: 44-1445-771-237

Duncan and Mhairi Mackenzie
The Sheiling Guest House
Garve Road
Ullapool, Wester Ross IV26 2SX, Scotland
Phone: 44-1854-612-947

The Ceilidh Place
14 West Argyle Street
Ullapool, Wester Ross IV26 2TY, Scotland
Phone: 44-1854-612-103
Fax: 44-1845-612-886
E-mail: reservations@ceilidh.demon.co.uk

Gerry and Mark Irvine
Summer Isles Hotel
Achiltibuie, Ross-shire IV26 2YG, Scotland
Phone: 44-1854-622-282
Fax: 44-1854-622-282
E-mail: summerisleshotel@aol.com

Lesley Crosfield and Colin Craig
The Albannach
Baddidarroch, Lochinver, Sutherland IV27 4LP, Scotland
Phone: 44-1571-844-407
Fax: 44-1571-844-285E-mail:
the.albannach@virgin.net

Penny Hawker
Scourie Lodge
Scourie, by Lairg, Sutherland IV27 4TE , Scotland
Phone: 44-1971-502-248

Lesley Black
Port-Na-Con Guest House
Loch Eriboll, by Lairg, Sutherland IV27 4UN , Scotland
Tel/Fax: 44-1971-511-367
E-mail: portnacon70@hotmail.com

INTERNET WEB SITES

WORLD WIDE WEB SOURCES are growing exponentially There is now even www.romantic-scotland.com if you need help with "romantic breaks, weddings, honeymoons, stag and hen parties." Much can be found by asking Google or Yahoo or Jeeves. Following are several sites I found most useful. The "www" has been left off of the site addresses.

host.co.uk The official site of the Highlands of Scotland Tourist Board. It provides events, see and do, accommodations (online reservations), travel info and useful links to other sites.

celticfringe.org.uk This "Guide to Wester Ross in North-West Scotland" is produced by the Celtic Fringe Tourism Association and is one of the best sites you will find. It includes online tours of Loch Maree, Loch Gairloch, Loch Ewe and other villages in the area. The site also provides external links to community web sites and various providers of boating, fishing, hiking and other activities.

highlandwelcome.co.uk Created by the Loch Ewe Action Form as a guide to the Loch Ewe area of Wester Ross—history, outdoor activities, accommodations, community activities and external links to 62 community, commercial and other sites.

tartans.com/landmark/thenorthcoast.html The north coast is one of several chapters of the Landmark Visitors Guide. The site combines history with a sharp-eyed appraisal of current sights and condition, town-by-town.

scotland-info.co.uk "The Internet Guide to Scotland" offers a good bit of history and just about everything else, for communities and surrounding areas.

musicscotland.com This covers the traditional music scene. Also try **ceolas.org**.

northern-times.co.uk The most northern newspaper published in Great Britain.

In addition to the sites listed above there are many community sites with a local flavor, including a schedule of town meetings and ceilidhs: **summerisles.com**; **achiltibuie.net**; **gairloch.co.uk**; **lochinver.net**; *and* **durness.org** (including the story of John Lennon's boyhood holidays on a croft in the Durness area with his cousin Stan).

ordnancesurvey.co.uk for absolutely wonderful maps. See below.

Hard Copy Sources and Guidebooks

British Tourist Authority, 551 Fifth Ave., New York, NY 101761-800-462-2748, to order publications published by the Highlands of Scotland Tourist Board: (1) *The Freedom of the Highlands*, a "list of quality assured accommodations," that, in addition to ratings (stars), includes access indicators at three levels—walks with cane, unassisted wheelchair and assisted wheelchair;(2) *Scotland Vacation Planner*; and (3) very complete "Where to Stay Guides"—*Scotland, Hotels & Guest Houses* and *Scotland Bed & Breakfast*.

The Highlands of Scotland Tourist Board
Peffery House. Strathpeffer, Ross-shire IV14 9HA
Phone: 011-44-1997-421-160; Fax: 1997-421-160
E-mail: admin@host.co.uk

Scottish Highlands & Islands: The Rough Guide
Rob Humphreys and Donald Reid, principal writers, provide more insight, more background, and far better writing than most guide-books, particularly for the landscape, seascape, and communities along the Atlantic Seaboard.

Scotland the Best! The One True Guide
Like opinion surveys, compiler Peter Irvine should admit to a margin of error. The book is not gospel, but it is useful for making one's own checklist.

Ordnance Survey Maps
Suggestion—start with *Road Map 1: Northern Scotland* at a scale of one inch to four miles. Later you can move on to the *Landranger* series at a scale of one inch to one mile. Maps can be ordered from Ordnance Survey in Great Britain at 011-44-1233-211-108 or on the Ordnance web site, www.ordnancesurvey.co.uk. Maps can be reviewed and printed at very small scale from that site.

BACKGROUND READING

The Scottish Nation: 1700-2000, T.M. Devine, Professor and Director of the Research Institute of Irish and Scottish Studies at the University of Aberdeen. A remarkably lucid and well-written book that puts facts and feelings about the sweep of Scottish history in perspective.

Insight Guide: Scotland (Third Edition). The front end of this book includes several highly informative essays, written in popular styles, by scholarly authors: "The Scottish Character" and "Beginnings," Brian Bell; "The Making of Modern Scotland," George Rosie; "Highlanders and Low Landers," T.C. Smout; and "How the Kirk Moulds Minds," Naomi May. There is a paragraph by Brian Bell in his essay, "Beginnings," that I have wanted to use somewhere in the book, but couldn't find a place until now. Dealing with the narrative of Scottish history, Bell writes:

> Summarize some of the stories and they seem more histrionic than historical. A sexy young widow returns from the French court to occupy the throne of Scotland, lays claim to the throne of England, conducts a series of passionate affairs, marries her lover a few weeks after he has allegedly murdered her second husband, loses the throne, is incarcerated for 19 years by her cousin, the Queen of England, and is then, on a pretext, beheaded. No soap-opera scriptwriter today would dare to invent as outrageous a plot as the true-life story of Mary Queen of Scots.

We Have Won The Land, John MacAskill. This is the story of the purchase of the North Lochinver Estate by the Assynt Crofters' Trust, a pioneering effort. The book bridges past and present in the crofters' struggle for subsistence and dignity.

APPENDIX II

HISTORY OF THE CROFT— LIFE, LAND, AND LAW

LOVE OF THE LAND, subsistence living, tribal and clan society, the deep wound of the clearances, crofting as a way of life—these historic strands are tied now to cultural and economic efforts to sustain unique communities and a way of life. How did it begin and what has it come to?

The Celts came from Ireland in the fifth century and established a small Scots kingdom. In 864, after some 400 years of fighting with the Picts, the King of the Scots, Kenneth MacAlpine, became king of Scots and Picts. This led to the domination of Gaelic language and culture in the whole of Alba, as Scotland was then known. This was a tribal society and all land was held in common by all members of the tribe.

Two hundred years on, beginning in 1057 with Malcolm Canmore (who forcibly replaced Macbeth) on the throne, southern influences came to dominate. A feudal system of lord and vassal and grants of land to individuals replaced the earlier common ownership. The king as owner of all lands made grants of his land by charter to subjects in return for military and other services, such as assassinating an enemy. Many of the grants were to incomers from the south. Scotland became a country of baronies, large freehold estates owned by "foreigners."

After the eighteen-year (1296 to1314) Scotland vs. England "wars" of independence, the Scottish victors "reallocated" most of the land to

Scottish patriots. This was the beginning of the clan society, a form of distributed aristocracy. The Scottish king gives you an estate that on your death is passed on to your children and by them to their children and so on. You are the clan chief and everyone who lives in your territory accepts your authority. In return, they expect your protection and land they can work. As clan chief, you want as many clansmen as possible to fight for "their" clan, because other clan chiefs are trying to take over your territory and you are trying to take over theirs in a winner-take-all approach to survival.

Genealogy charts of the period make for bloody reading. The MacLeods of Assynt offer a good example. Clan chief Houchan, born in 1524, had five sons and one daughter. Neil the Tutor killed Houchan. Then Houchan's son Neil killed Alexander and was in turn killed by Angus, son of Alexander; son Donald was killed by Neil the Tutor; son John was killed by Donald Ban; son Rory was killed by Donald Ban; son Angus killed Norman, son of Neil, and was then executed by Donald Ban; and daughter Helen was abducted by Aodh Dubh MacKay of Farr.

By the seventeenth century, surviving clan chiefs had well established territories and gave permanent leases of land to sons or other close relatives, known then as "tacksmen." Tacksmen in turn sublet most of their land to clan members who were "tenants at will." They could be moved about, but it was understood that as members of the clan they would always be provided with land. Tenants worked the land in groups in a "run-rig'" system. Land was divided into strips that were rotated each year, so in theory, each tenant had a share of better and poorer land. It was a life of bare subsistence. Turf or stone homes were more often than not shared with chickens and cattle. But, as Katharine Stewart wrote in *Crofts and Crofting*, "While the life was harsh people felt secure in their kinship with one another and their clan chief . . . All were assured of a rough and ready justice meted out by the head of the clan in any dispute." These were a people, "sensitive to their world in all its aspects, living a close-knit communal life and passionately attached to their glens and hills."

In the early eighteenth century after the union with England (viewed by most Scots as a shotgun marriage), several forces eroded the bonds of clanship and began the transformation of Highland life. One force was an intellectual, scientific, and mercantile phenomenon, the Scottish Enlightenment. Edinburgh was becoming one of the intellectual powerhouses of Western Europe. New ideas, new roads, and new ambitions penetrated the Highland fastness and clan chiefs found a new and larger world opening up to them. Social life in the Lowlands was expensive, and to be players, clan chiefs needed money. Land and control over the lives of tenants were their principal assets. Transforming these assets into profits and ready cash changed clanship from mutual obligations between clan chief and clansman to a commercial relationship of landlord and tenant.

Other forces reshaping the Highlands were the destruction of the clan as a military organization with the defeat of Bonnie Prince Charlie and the Highlanders at Culloden in 1746, and the demands of developing industries in Lowland Scotland and England for products the Highlands could supply. Need and opportunity merged. Chiefs/landlords needed money and they could get it by changing the ways land was used, and the work tenants could be forced to perform.

Assynt provides an example. Here tenants were torn from their glens and hills and cleared to coastal crofts in two waves, in 1812 and 1819. Landlords profited in several ways. Cleared lands increased in value when used as large sheep pastures, yielding wool for mills in the south. Tennant crofts, small holdings of enclosed land with a share in common grazing, were of poor quality and small size. In addition to working poor land, a crofter was forced to work at other jobs that benefited the landlord. One job was fishing. Another was kelp making—the collection and burning of seaweed to make alginate, used at that time to make glass and soap. Twenty tons of seaweed collected by hand produced one ton of ash. It was brutal, exhausting work.

Together, landlord profits came from four sources—wool, fishing, alginate and rents paid by crofters. If crofters improved their land, draining and fertilizing it or adding a barn, their rent would be increased. Estate factors (managers) had "awesome powers of eviction" since tenants held their crofts on a year-to-year basis. Crofters in one area were said to be in "such a state of slavish fear" they dared not complain about their grievances. Crofter Donald MacAskill testified before the Napier Commission, "I am ashamed to confess it now that I trembled more before the factor than I did before the Lord of Lords." The bitterness of those times is a legacy that remains today. A more positive legacy is the communal pattern of life and interdependence of close-knit crofting communities where people still look after one another.

The plight of crofters became a national issue. Famines devastated the land. Land seizures by crofters and other acts of open rebellion came to be known as the "land wars." Agitation grew in the radical press, especially with the example of the Irish Land Act of 1881 that provided small farmers in Ireland security of tenure and fair rents. According to T.M. Devine, all these factors brought crofter's rights in the Highlands to a boil and the "current of political and public opinion was flowing fast against the landed interest."

In 1883 a Royal Commission headed by Lord Napier held hearings on the condition of crofters. These hearings, continuing agitation by crofters, and growing national outrage led Gladstone's government in 1888 to pass the Crofters Holdings (Scotland) Act. It stripped landlords of many rights of ownership and began a new era in crofter rights. Now, security of tenure for crofters was guaranteed as long as they paid their rent. Fair rents could be fixed by a land court. Crofters were to be paid for improvements if they gave up their croft or were removed. Crofts were heritable, that is, they could be passed on to children or relatives. In effect the "sacred rights" of private property had been breached and government was now a partner in crofter-landlord relations.

The Crofters Holdings Act was a beginning, but it did not quiet the agitation of crofters for land of their own, much less enough to subsist on. The Highlands Congested Districts Board was created in 1897, providing funds for roads, fisheries, fencing, draining and other improvements that benefited both landlords and crofters. In 1911, the Small Landholders (Scotland) Act established the Scottish Land Court, to which appeal could be made in case of excessive rents. In 1919, the Land Settlement (Scotland) Bill granted the Board of Agriculture rights of "compulsory purchase" of land when required to resolve crofter and landlord conflicts. By the late 1920s, emigration overseas and to the cities had reduced the Highland population and much of the pressure for land.

With changes in expectations after World War II, the need for ancillary jobs other than fishing and weaving and various other forms of support became obvious if crofting was to survive. The emphasis of public policy began shifting beyond fairness and equity to encompass survival of a way of life. In 1954 a commission of inquiry into crofting conditions argued, "The crofting system deserves to be maintained if only for the reason that it supports a free and independent way of life which in a civilization predominantly urban and industrial in character is worth preserving for its own intrinsic quality."

The Crofters (Scotland) Act of 1955 followed, creating a Crofters' Commission to "sustain the economic basis and way of life of crofting communities and help retain population in crofting areas." By 2001 the Commission was providing £2,617,000 ($3,800,000) a year in agricultural grants to crofts for land improvement, fencing, agricultural buildings and farm equipment. A Croft Entrance Scheme was designed to bring younger people into crofting. Of these new entrants, 88 percent are now second or third generation children of croft families.

In the last several years £5,800,000 ($8,400,000) in seed money has gone into a Crofting Township Development Scheme that encourages community projects ranging from community halls to TV masts and tourist information centers. One such project was the Coigach Community Hall in Achiltibuie that also received financial support from the Highland Council, the Millennium Commission, the Scottish Executive, and Ross & Cromarty Enterprise, this last another new agency aimed at the creation of non-agricultural jobs for crofters and their families.

From a beginning when tribes and clans took care of their own, we now see a lot of players on the scene in current efforts to support crofters and sustain crofting townships, "fragile rural communities," as a way of life.

GAELIC: PRONUNCIATION AND TERMS

THERE ARE FOUR CELTIC languages spoken today—Welsh, Irish, Breton, and Scottish Gaelic (Gaidhlig, pronounced "Gallic" as in gal or gallon). Introduced from Ireland around the third century BC, Gaelic grew to be the national language of Scotland. In the twelfth century, Gaelic began to give way as the church, commerce, and wealth passed into non-Gaelic hands. The Union of Scotland and England accelerated the decline and public policy enforced it. The 1872 Education Act ignored Gaelic and students were punished if caught speaking it in school.

There are now about 90,000 Gaelic speakers, only two percent of the Scottish population, and another 250,000 who understand the language. Most who speak or know Gaelic live in the Hebrides and the North West Highlands. There is now something of a renaissance in the language with bilingual pre-school and primary schools, Gaelic language courses in secondary schools, a major increase in Gaelic-language broadcasting, and the mass audience for Gaelic music. Many road signs in the Highlands are in both English and Gaelic.

Whatever the status of Gaelic usage today, the names of townships, villages, mountains, and lochs are virtually all in the Gaelic of an earlier day.

ALPHABET AND PRONUNCIATION

AS EXPLAINED ON www.contemporarypoetry.com, there are eighteen letters in Gaelic. Of these, five are vowels (a, e, i, o, and u as in English), one is the letter "h", which is in a category all by itself, and the remaining letters are consonants (b, c, d, f, g, l, m, n, p, r, s, and t). Of the vowels, two (e and i) are called "slender" vowels, and three (a,o,u) are called "broad" vowels. All consonants except l, n, and r can become aspirated in writing, and this changes their sound as well. (Aspirate: pronounced with an exhalation of breath with the sound of h.) L, n, and r also sound different when aspirated in speech, but this is not marked in writing. To aspirate a letter, you simply put "h" after it when it appears at the beginning of a word.

Here are some examples from *The Rough Guide*.

Short and long vowels: short—a as in cat but after nn or l like ow in bow; long—`a as in bar; short—o as in pot; long—`o like the a in enthrall.

Vowel combinations: ai like the a in cat, or the e in pet but before dh or gh, like the ee in street; ao like the ur in surly; ei like the a in mate; ea like the e in pet, or the a in cat and sometimes like the a in mate, but before ll or nn, like the ow in bow (of a boat).

Consonants: **b** at the beginning of a word as in big, but in the middle or at the end of a word like the p in pair; **g** at the beginning of a word as in get, before e like the y in yes, in the middle or end of a word like the ck in sock and after i like the ch in loch.

Aspirated consonants: **bh** at the beginning of a word is like the v in van, elsewhere it is silent; **gh** at the beginning of a word as in get but before or after a, o, or u, rather like someone gargling and after an i, sometimes like the y in gay, but often silent.

For more than this on Gaelic pronunciation, I suggest you go to the Internet for an online course. See, for example, www.contemporarypoetry.com/brain/lang/scots1.html.

Terms, Mostly of Gaelic Origin

THIS BRIEF GLOSSARY COVERS terms used in this book. Many of the terms form a part of place names.

Aber	Mouth of a river
Ach, Auch	Field
Allt, Alt, Ault	Burn or stream
Aird	Promontory or high point
Bad	Cluster
Bal	Homestead
Bealach	Pass, gap
Beg, Beag	Small, little
Beinn, Ben	Mountain
Binnean	Pinnacle, conical hill
Camas	Bay, creek or harbor
Cnoc	Little hill
Clach	Stone, stone weight
Coll	Wood
Creag	Rock, cliff
Cul	The back
Dearg	Red, violet, impetuous
Drem, Drum	Ridge
Dubh	Blacken, blot out
Dun	Hill, heap, fort
Eas	Waterfall
Eilean	Island
Gleann	Valley

Inch	Meadow, small island
Inver	Mouth of river
Kinloch	At the head of a lake
Kyle	Narrow strait
Loch	Inland lake, sea inlet
Lochan	Small lake
Mor, More	Large, great
Ness	Cape, headland (Norse)
Pol, Poll	Pit, hole, mire
Rubha, Rhu	Promontory
Sgurr	Peak, pointed rock
Stac	Steep projecting rock
Stack	Columnar rock (Norse)
Strath	Broad valley
Tarbet	Isthmus
Tigh	House

Place Names and Their English Meaning

THIS LIST INCLUDES MANY of the place names used in this book and their English meaning.

Achmelvich	Field of the sand dunes
Achiltibuie	Field of the golden boy
Ardvreck	Speckled point
Assynt	Ridge end
Badnaban	Grove of the women
Ben Mor Coigach	Big mountain of the fifth part
Ben More Assynt	Big mountain of Assynt
Clachtoll	Split stone
Coigach	Place of the fifth part
Cul Beag	Small back

Culkein	Back of the headland
Cul Mor	Big back
Drumbeg	Little ridge
Eas a' Chual Aluinn	Fine waterfall
Glas Bheinn	Gray mountain
Inchnadamph	Riverside field of the ox
Inverkirkaig	Church at the mouth of the river
Kylesku	Narrows
Ledmore	Big slope
Loch an Leothard	Loch of the steep hill
Loch Borralan	Loch of the waves
Loch Dubh	Dark loch
Lochinver	Sea loch at the river mouth
Loch Lurgainn	Shank loch
Nedd	Nest
Polbain	White pool
Quinag	Milking pail
Sgurr an Fhidhleir	Peak of the fiddler
Spidean Coinich	Mossy peak
Stac Pollaidh	Steep hill of the peat bog
Stoer (Viking)	Large stack

NOTES

INTRODUCTION

xviii "A time when Scotland . . .": *The Scottish Nation 1700 – 2000*, T.M. Devin, Penguin Books (2000), p. ix

xix   " . . . a middle class holiday . . .": *Scottish Highlands & Islands: The Rough Guide* (2000), p. 271

xx   "The ancient and significant . . .": *Insight Guide: Scotland*, Houghton Mifflin Company (1995), "Highlands and Lowlands," T.C. Smout, p. 67

xxi   "The relationship between . . .": *Scotland* (see above), "How the Kirk Moulds Minds," Naomi May, p. 73

xxi   " . . . often unmodern in priorities . . .": Smout (see above), p. 68

CHAPTER 1

3   "There are all kinds of loyalties . . .": Donald Kennedy, "The New School Spirit," *New York Times*

3   " . . . supported by modest farming . . .": *Peoples & Settlements in North-West Ross*, Scottish Society for Northern Studies (1994), John R. Baldwin, p. xiii

CHAPTER 2

25   " . . . loch being black with ships . . .": www.freespace.virgin.net/
      leaf.ltd/wartime.html

CHAPTER 3

29   Quotations and statistics in the section "Ullapool and the
      Unfaithful Red Herring" are from the chapter "Ullapool and the
      British Fisheries Society," Jean Munro, *Peoples & Settlements* (cited
      above), pp. 244-270

38   "Women total 37.2% . . .": *Women in National Parliaments,*
      www.ipu.org/wmn-e/world.htm

CHAPTER 4

41-44 "Locals and Incomers: Social and Cultural Identity in Late
      Twentieth Century Coigach," Angus MacLeod and Geoff
      Payne, *Peoples & Settlements* (see above)—local/incomer distribu-
      tion, pp. 396-396; housing statistics, p. 399; deforcement,
      including Margaret MacLeod story, pp. 405-406

CHAPTER 6

71-72 "Over fifty townships . . .": quoted in *The Assynt Clearances,*
      Assynt Press (1998). Malcolm Bangor-Jones, p.1
72   "Destination of Households . . .": *The Assynt Clearances* (see
      above), p. 56

73-74 Purchase of the North Assynt Estate, quotations and factual data, *We Have Won The Land*, Acair Limited (1989), John MacAskill

75-77 Life, Land, and Law: principal sources for this section and Appendix II: *Crofts and Crofting*, Mercat Press (1980) and *The Scottish Nation* (see above), "The Highlands and Crofting Society," pp. 413-447

CHAPTER 7

83   Midget submarines: www.navalhistory.net/ww2britishshipssub-marines.htm

86   " . . .kingdom of twelve . . .": www.taighabhrazoin.freeserve.co.uk/handa.htm

Chapter 8

96-97 "The natives are generally . . .": *Durness Past and Present*, p. 2

98   Surrender: www.unclefed.com/funstuff/HistDocs/germsur3.html

99   Thrust Tectonics: www.earth.leeds.ac.uk/mtb/northernzone/eriboll

99   " . . . faceless, negligent . . .": *The Herald*, "Estate Thwarts Home Plan," January 27, 2000

99   ". . .will underpin the economy . . .": *TED Case Studies*, #229, "Scottish Quarry Trade"

102   " . . . a mourning and grateful . . .": quoted in *Highlands & Islands* (see above), p.272

INDEX

About the Author

Born in Detroit in 1926, Warren Rovetch completed his undergraduate studies at Wayne University in Detroit, and graduate studies at Oxford (Balliol College), where he was a Sir Robert Mayer Fellow and Fulbright Scholar, receiving his M. Phil. in economics in 1950.

Rovetch has been a government economist, an industrial engineer, a regional director for the Foreign Policy Association, and a consultant to colleges and universities. The first of his many entrepreneurial enterprises was Education Research Associates, where he created a Denver center for dropouts and directed a study of post secondary education for the Colorado Legislature. His next step was Campus Facilities Associates, with a focus on campus planning and studies of institutional priorities. Foundations for Learning—the next company he started—published textbooks and trained teachers to achieve a new paradigm of teaching and learning, and was acquired by Simon & Schuster.

Rovetch then went on to establish Columbia River Properties and developed an environmentally based education and tour center on the Lewis and Clark Water Trail of the Lower Columbia River.

His travels began in 1946, his pre-creaky days, with a yearlong adventure through six countries of war-torn Europe. In England he spent nearly six months giving current events talks for the United States Information Agency and lectures on American history for a British army officers, training program. Over the rest of the twentieth century and into the twenty-first, Rovetch and his wife of fifty years made twenty-five extended trips to Europe and effected the transition from traveler to Creaky Traveler.

To share your Creaky experiences, you can get in touch with Warren Rovetch at warrenrovetch@msn.com.

Sentient Publications, LLC publishes books on cultural creativity, experimental education, transformative spirituality, holistic health, new science, ecology, and other topics, approached from an integral viewpoint. Our authors are intensely interested in exploring the nature of life from fresh perspectives, addressing life's great questions, and fostering the full expression of the human potential. Sentient Publications' books arise from the spirit of inquiry and the richness of the inherent dialogue between writer and reader.

Our Culture Tools series is designed to give social catalyzers and cultural entrepreneurs the essential information, technology, and inspiration to forge a sustainable, creative, and compassionate world.

We are very interested in hearing from our readers. To direct suggestions or comments to us, or to be added to our mailing list, please contact:

SENTIENT PUBLICATIONS, LLC
1113 Spruce Street
Boulder, CO 80302
303-443-2188
contact@sentientpublications.com
www.sentientpublications.com